PRACTICAL
HARMONY

PRACTICAL HARMONY

An Integrated Course in the Principles of

HARMONIC-MELODIC WRITING,

KEYBOARD IMPROVISATION, AND MODULATION

By

HANS TISCHLER

Roosevelt University

BOSTON : ALLYN AND BACON, INC.

1 9 6 4

CONTENTS

part I : Fundamentals

part II : Diatonic Harmony

part III : Chromatic Harmony and Modulation

PRACTICAL
HARMONY

INTRODUCTION:
SCOPE AND PURPOSES

a : WHAT DOES THE STUDY OF HARMONY ACCOMPLISH?

Every music student knows that he has to study harmony, but he rarely understands the importance and practical value of this study. Only when he discovers that musical "theory" is really an eminently practical pursuit will he be able to derive the proper benefit from it by applying the materials he has learned to actual musical situations which he will encounter. It may be helpful at the start, then, to explain briefly what the student may expect to gain from the study of harmony.

What is known as "style" in music is the result of the combination and characteristic use of certain basic elements: rhythm, melody, harmony, counterpoint, tone color, expression (tempo, dynamics, and tone production), non-musical content (such as text, program, or historical situation), and structure, or form. Of these, only the first four are involved in the present study, the third most fully; the last four fall entirely outside the scope of this book and must be reserved for subsequent study. Since all or most of the eight elements are employed in any composition, a harmony course does not and cannot teach the craft of composing. This limitation is often not clearly understood by students, who are consequently disappointed by this fascinating discipline.

In fact, a study such as this cannot possibly encompass all varieties of even the first four elements; many, indeed, remain to be discovered. The student must first learn to understand and use those varieties that have been accepted as standard, regular, or fundamental approaches because of their frequency in the works of the great masters of the eighteenth and nineteenth centuries. Only when these have become, like basic grammar and syntax in language, a firm core of the student's musical education, can he use or understand their characteristic modifications and derivations which constitute the individual styles of the composers. Basic music theory is always the result of analyzing the techniques of the past and does not regulate original creative effort, although it guides it.

A study of harmony deals with:

1. The workings of the Major/Minor system regarding
   a. Key signatures and possible deviations
   b. Scales and chords in each key and possible deviations
   c. Transposition
   d. Modulation

2. The use of the Major/Minor system made by the composers of the eighteenth and nineteenth centuries with respect to all items listed under (1) as well as to achieving
   a. Cadences and phrases
   b. Accompaniments for melodies, particularly simple ones such as those for hymns and folk songs
   c. Harmonic or tonal coherence in compositions, particularly in short works such as songs and small piano pieces

In addition, the study of harmony will help the student to (1) recognize the tonality of a piece of music and the significance of non-harmonic tones in it, aiding him in detailed artistic interpretation; (2) identify scale fragments, chords, and nonharmonic tones in singing and playing, leading to a facility in sight singing, sight reading, and memorizing; (3) transpose on the piano, a skill needed in teaching and score reading; (4) improvise on the piano and organ, freely or when accompanying; and (5) analyze the structure of musical works, the all-important basis of over-all artistic interpretation.

To achieve these results fully, much study and practice is necessary, some of which goes beyond a harmony course; for the study of harmony produces primarily an understanding of the various problems we have listed, while practical application depends upon continuous exercise and use of these understandings in other musical studies, particularly in vocal and instrumental ones.

b : THE ORDER AND METHOD OF PRESENTATION

This book does not deal with contemporary techniques: its goal is to state clearly the principles of the harmonic practices of the eighteenth and nineteenth centuries. It is based squarely on the pedagogy of *functional harmony* and explains the harmonic phenomena in terms of root progressions, or Jean Philippe Rameau's "fundamental bass." This traditional system, as taught from Rameau (1683–1764) to Heinrich Schenker (1868–1935), places its emphasis on the functioning of dominants and substitute harmonies within a key and in this way differs from contemporary music with its lack, or complete negation, of such an emphasis.

During the period from about 1600 to 1900 the harmonic cadence constituted the basic framework of the musical phrase. The evolution of harmonic style during that period may be described as follows: (1) the establishment of the cadence and of tonality (1600–1670); (2) the variegation of the cadence with the inclusion of more diatonic steps (1670–1720); (3) the introduction of secondary dominants and cadences and the establishment of key regions for the purpose of planning large forms (1720–1760); (4) the development of diatonic modulation and key contrasts and the establishment of the musical sentence or period (1760–1800); (5) the introduction of modal mixtures and chromatic mediants for the enrichment of the cadence (1800–1850); (6) the development of linear alterations and chromatic and enharmonic modulation (1850–1900), exploiting very distant tonal relationships and leading to a loosening of the tonal framework of the music of that period. This book will proceed from a discussion of the basic skills in reading and writing music and playing it on the keyboard through the first two phases we have outlined. Then the other phases will be discussed, though not necessarily in the preceding order, because the purpose here is not a historical but a pedagogical one.

No book can possibly supplant the guidance of an imaginative teacher. What this book tries to do is to supply the most important explanations and exercises in a well-ordered sequence. In most cases it will probably not be necessary to do all the exercises, but from each group several should be worked out. In any event, the student should practice all the keyboard exercises, since only the very minimum have been included. Without them, written exercises tend to become an unmusical enterprise, more akin to solving crossword puzzles than to learning music. With the teacher's help, many exercises will also serve for ear training. Some of them may be used for sight singing as well, but more complete materials for sight singing are readily available elsewhere.

Although the chapters in this book are arranged in the order in which they are to be studied, it should be clearly understood that in some cases the study of a chapter must be continued concurrently with that of subsequent chapters. This is true especially of Chapters 2 (intervals), 4 (circles of fifths, harmonic and melodic Minors, and scales), and 5 (transposition). In fact, scales will have to be continuously practiced for many months to provide the basis for most subsequent chapters in this volume.

In this text rules are kept to an absolute minimum. For the sake of easy reference to the basic rules, procedures, and suggestions, they are all reprinted in the appendixes to Parts II and III. These rules should be taken for what they are: not natural laws, but socially determined rules of taste. In music, as in all human activities, taste is based on social norms, which change from period to period. Therefore, the rules that applied to the music of the eighteenth and nineteenth centuries do not apply without some modification to the music of other eras.

c : SYMBOLS

The following symbols and abbreviations are used throughout:

Major, Minor = major key, minor key (not chords, intervals,
(capitalized)   or scales)

A, B, etc.   = single tones, or A Major, B Major, etc.

a, b, etc.	= A Minor, B Minor, etc.
I, II, etc.	= major triad on the first, second, etc., scale steps
i, ii, etc.	= minor triad on the first, second, etc., scale steps
III⁺	= augmented triad on the third scale step
ii°, vii°	= diminished triads on the second and seventh scale steps
a	= augmented; anticipation
A	= appoggiatura
d	= diminished
D	= dominant
D/	= dominant of
ll	= left by leap
m	= minor
M	= major
N6	= Neapolitan six-chord
op.	= operation
p	= perfect; passing tone
P	= pedal point
pos.	= position
r	= root
rl	= reached by leap
S	= subdominant; suspension
t	= turning tone
BR	= Bach-Riemenschneider, *371 Harmonized Chorales and 69 Chorale Melodies with Figured Bass* (New York: G. Schirmer, Inc., 1941)
HC	= Thomas W. Surette and Archibald T. Davison, *The Home and Community Song Book* (Boston: E. C. Schirmer Music Co., 1931)

I

FUNDAMENTALS

1

NOTATION

a : NOTE AND REST VALUES

Music, like poetry, may be transmitted from generation to generation aurally, and much religious and folk music is still passed on in this way today. However, the increasing complexity of art music, as well as its expanding popularity, led musicians in Europe and other advanced cultures to turn to written symbols, which made transmission and learning easier and gave the music greater permanence.

In developing a system of music writing, or *notation*, the problem was to find symbols which would give information about both the relative pitches and relative durations of musical tones. When Western notation was started around the year 800, musicians found symbols to indicate pitch only, for these symbols, the *neumes*, were used for the teaching of the single-voiced or *monophonic* Gregorian chants, the flow of whose tones was rather free. But about four centuries later, when music for several simultaneous voices, or *polyphony*, rose, it became necessary to coordinate these voices by indicating the comparative length of sounds and silences, and a new measured or *mensural* notation was developed from which our modern symbols derive.

The various durations of sounds and silences are symbolized respectively by types of *notes* and *rests*, which are said to be of various *values*. Each note or rest value is related to the next shorter one as $1 : \frac{1}{2}$. In other words, they are all divisible by two only, as follows:

Name	Note symbol	When connected in groups of two or more	Rest symbol
$\frac{2}{1}$ *breve* (double whole)	𝄺		𝄽
$\frac{1}{1}$ *whole-note* (semibreve)	𝅝		𝄼
$\frac{1}{2}$ *half-note* (minim)	𝅗𝅥 or ρ		𝄼
$\frac{1}{4}$ *quarter-note* (crotchet)	𝅘𝅥 or ρ		𝄽
$\frac{1}{8}$ *eighth-note* (quaver)	𝅘𝅥𝅮 or ρ	𝅘𝅥𝅮𝅘𝅥𝅮 or 𝅘𝅥𝅮𝅘𝅥𝅮	𝄾
$\frac{1}{16}$ *sixteenth-note* (semiquaver)	𝅘𝅥𝅯 or ρ	𝅘𝅥𝅯𝅘𝅥𝅯 or 𝅘𝅥𝅯𝅘𝅥𝅯	𝄿
$\frac{1}{32}$ *thirty-second-note* (demisemiquaver)	𝅘𝅥𝅰 or ρ	𝅘𝅥𝅰𝅘𝅥𝅰 or 𝅘𝅥𝅰𝅘𝅥𝅰	𝅀
$\frac{1}{64}$ *sixty-fourth-note* (hemidemisemiquaver)	𝅘𝅥𝅱 or ρ	𝅘𝅥𝅱𝅘𝅥𝅱 or 𝅘𝅥𝅱𝅘𝅥𝅱	𝅁

The parts of each note are named as follows:

The straightened-out flag that serves to connect several eighth-notes or smaller note values is called a *beam*. Observe that the note head is not round but oval and tilts upward from left to right. To avoid the laborious filling-in, black note heads are best handwritten as obliquely ascending bars: ♩, ♪. Stems are drawn downward on the left side of the head and upward on its right side, but the flags are always drawn on the right side of the stem and in opposite direction to it: ♪, ♪. There is the same number of flags in notes and rests of the same value; for example, there are two flags in a sixteenth-note and in a sixteenth-rest.

Since music requires a greater variety of length relationships than $1 : \frac{1}{2}$, two further devices are used: the *dot* and the *tie*.

A dot which is written after a note head or a rest gives this symbol one and one-half times its usual length, or, the value of three rather than two of the next shorter note or rest value. Thus 𝅝 = 𝅗𝅥 𝅗𝅥 , whereas 𝅝· = 𝅗𝅥 𝅗𝅥 𝅗𝅥 ; or 𝄽 = 𝄾 𝄾 , whereas 𝄽· = 𝄾 𝄾 𝄾 . This lengthening dot may be used with any note or rest value, though it is rarely written after whole and breve rests.

The tie is a bow or slur that connects two note heads. It enables us to express note values totaling various combinations of equal smaller note values (five, seven, nine, and so on) that cannot be symbolized by either simple or dotted single notes. For example: ♪♪· = ♫ ♬ , and 𝅗𝅥· 𝅗𝅥· = ♬♬♬ . Rests need no ties; they are simply written one after another: 𝄽 𝄾· = 𝄾 𝄾 𝄾 𝄾 𝄾 𝄾 . (For other uses of the tie see Chapter 3, section b.)

EXERCISES

1. Write a single note of the value of

2♪, 3♬, 4♩, 6♩, 8♬, 2♩.

2. Use two notes and a tie to represent a single value of

5♩, 3♩·, 7♪, 11♬, 13♬, 6♪·, 15♬

3. Write rests equivalent to

♩·, ♩ ♩·, ♩· ♪·, ♪, ♩ ♬, 𝅝·, 𝅜·

b : STAFF AND COMMON CLEFS

To symbolize the ups and downs of melody, medieval scribes at first used wavy lines and dots — neumes. Since these yielded only approximations of the actual distances between notes, musicians began to draw straight lines across the page and traced the neumes within them, pinpointing the various pitches by thickening the neumes in the appropriate places. The thickening of the neumes developed into the note heads, while the connecting hair lines became the stems. In front of the lines, which later consolidated into the *staff* (plural: *staves*), the alphabetic note names from A to G were written, and these eventually became the *clefs*.

The musical staff has five lines (except in Gregorian chants, where it has only four), counted from the lowest to the highest, and four spaces. Each of these nine positions, as well as those added by short *ledger lines* above or below the staff when needed, is reserved for a specific pitch corresponding to one of the alphabetic note names and to a white key on the piano. The ascending alphabetic series (A to G) of these note names always remains the same, but a clef is necessary to determine where the series starts, or which particular pitch is designated by a note on a certain line or in a certain space.

Today only three of the seven note names are used as clefs. Formerly each of these names could be placed at the head of any line, but today two of them are always placed on a single line, and the third occurs in only two positions. They are:

1. The *treble*, or *G*, *clef*, always curling around the second line, developed from an embroidered G:

2. The *bass*, or *F*, *clef*, always outlining the fourth line with its two dots, developed from an embroidered F:

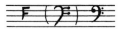

3. The *C clef*, called *alto clef* when it centers on the third line and *tenor clef* when it centers on the fourth. This clef assumes several shapes, all derived from an embroidered C:

The C clef occurs only in orchestral and choral scores, never on the piano. It indicates the middle C, which is the C nearest the center of the piano. The usual piano score contains two staves: one for the right hand with a treble clef and one for the left hand with a bass clef, signifying respectively the G above the middle C and the F below it. Within such a *grand staff* the C clef would occupy an imaginary eleventh line midway between the two five-line staves.

With the aid of these clefs the same pitch may be symbolized in several different ways. For example, the middle C may be written:

But whatever the symbol, the note above that C will always be D, the one in the space below it will be a B, and so on. Regardless of clef, the breve, whole, and half rests are usually written between the third and fourth lines, while the other rests cross the third line:

EXERCISES

1. a. Write the D above middle C and the B below it in all four clefs.

   b. Do the same with E above and A below middle C, then with F above and G below.

2. a. Write G and C above middle C in the treble, alto, and tenor clefs.

   b. Write F and C below middle C in the alto, tenor, and bass clefs.

c : ACCIDENTALS

With the notes discussed up to here we can represent only those pitches that correspond to the white keys on the piano. These notes must be modified to apply to the other pitches also, those represented by the black keys. Such modifications are brought about by four signs called *accidentals*. They are:

1. ♯ (*sharp*), which indicates the pitch just above the note it modifies, produced on the piano by the key directly to its right (or one half-tone up from it)

2. ✗ or ✲ (*double sharp*), which indicates the pitch just above the foregoing, produced on the piano by the second key to the right (or one whole-tone up)

3. ♭ (*flat*), which indicates the pitch just below the note it modifies, produced on the piano by the key directly to its left (or one half-tone down from it)

4. ♭♭ (*double flat*), which indicates the pitch just below the foregoing, produced on the piano by the second key to the left (or one whole-tone down)

These signs are all written before the note head which they modify. The following example shows the note C and its four possible modifications with their positions on the keyboard:

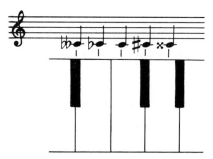

This example clearly shows that an accidental does not necessarily indicate a black key, although without accidentals we could not refer to any black key.

When a note is raised or lowered by an accidental and then returns in the music without being modified, the musician uses a *cancel* or *natural* (♮) to restore the note to its original meaning.

Although all five signs are written before the note, in talking we put the name of the modifier after that of the note. We speak of the five notes in the preceding example as C-double-flat, C-flat, C-natural, C-sharp, and C-double-sharp.

All the five signs are derived from the letter b, which in medieval music was written round, "b," to indicate what today is called B-flat, and square, "♮," to indicate our B-natural. The latter sign split into the natural and sharp signs, and by writing the last obliquely, "𝄪," the double sharp was developed.

EXERCISES

1. Write the following notes in all four clefs: E♭ and F♯ above middle C, B♭ and G♯ below middle C. Play these notes on the piano.

2. Play the following notes on the piano:

3. Write the following notes in treble, alto, and tenor clefs: G𝄪 and B♭♭ above middle C, and F𝄪 and E♭♭ below. Play these notes on the piano.

d : OTTAVA SIGNS

The distance or *interval* between any note and the one nearest to it that bears the same name (for instance, between one C and the next C up or down) is called an *octave*. Using both staves of the piano grand staff and a few ledger lines, we can write notes for all white and black keys for a range of four octaves:

There are, however, eight octaves in our musical system. In order to write all possible notes, we employ a simple sign called the *ottava sign:*

8va - - - ⌐
                   or
               8va - - - ⌐

The former, written above a note or a passage, directs us to play whatever is beneath it an octave higher; the latter, written below a note or
a passage, indicates that what is so marked is to be played an octave
lower.   Here are some examples:

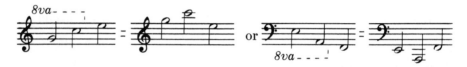

The octave sign often appears merely as 8. . . . , and a shift of two
octaves may be indicated by 15. . . . .

e : NAMES OF OCTAVES AND ENHARMONIC NOTES

Western music uses about eight octaves, of which the piano keyboard
usually contains seven and one-third.   In order to differentiate among
these octaves, each one (beginning with C and going up to B) has been
given a particular name.   The lowest tone on the piano is *subcontra* A,
or $_2$A.   The lowest C belongs to the *contra*-octave ($_1$C to $_1$B), from
which one ascends through the *great* (C to B), *small* (c to b), *one-line*
(c^1 to b^1), *two-line* (c^2 to b^2), *three-line* (c^3 to b^3), and *four-line* octaves
(c^4 to b^4) to the highest tone on the piano, *five-line C* (c^5) :†

† In some books symbols such as c^1 and a^3 are given as c′ and a‴.

Each octave contains twelve tones, but all of these may be written in two or three different ways, so that there are more than twelve notes in an octave. The various notes that may be used to indicate the same tone, such as F-sharp and G-flat or B and C-flat, are called *enharmonic*. The following table gives the twelve tones of an octave with their enharmonic spellings. Spellings that are rarely used are shown in parentheses.

A	Bb	B	C	C#	D	Eb	E	F	F#	G	G#
G✕	A#	(A✕)	B#	(B✕)	C✕	D#	(D✕)	E#	(E✕)	F✕	Ab
Bbb	(Cbb)	Cb	(Dbb)	Db	Ebb	(Fbb)	Fb	(Gbb)	Gb		Abb

EXERCISES

1. Sketch an octave of the piano keyboard and ascribe to each key its several names.

2. Write out C, E, and G in all octaves of the piano keyboard and ascribe their octave designations (for example, c^1 or $_1E$). Then play these notes on the piano and name them and their octaves aloud.

3. Write the following notes and play them on the piano:

    a. C   **c.** g#   **e.** $b\#^1$ **g.** $_2Bb$

    b. eb   **d.** $_1A$ **f.** db^4

4. Learn to play any given note in any named octave.

5. Play each of the following notes in each of the four given clefs:

2

INTERVALS

a : DEFINITION

An *interval* is the difference in pitch or the distance between two tones. Its numerical name indicates that distance and is found by counting the letter names of the notes from one tone to the other. Thus A to C is a third (A-B-C), even if the A is modified to A-flat or A-sharp, or the C to C-flat or C-sharp, or both are modified. Such modifications are noted by adjectives: perfect, major, minor, augmented, and diminished.

For historical reasons certain intervals are called *perfect*, namely, the prime, fourth, fifth, and octave, while others are called *imperfect*, namely, the second, third, sixth, and seventh. These labels do not mean what the words usually imply; they only indicate that perfect intervals appear ordinarily in only one size each, while imperfect intervals appear as either *major* or *minor*, the difference between these always being a *half-tone*, which is the interval between any tone on the piano and its nearest upper or lower neighbor. An interval with the same numerical name as a perfect or major interval, but which is a half-tone larger, is called *augmented*. An interval which is a half-tone smaller than a perfect or a minor interval is called *diminished*. Double augmented and double diminished intervals, though theoretically possible, occur very rarely.

Intervals which occur within an octave are called *simple intervals*, and a list of these follows, with some rare ones omitted. Intervals larger than an octave are called *compound*. Up to the double octave these are often given their own names (for example, the octave-plus-second is a ninth), but they take their adjectives — such as major, minor, or perfect — from the simple intervals by which they exceed the octave, double octave, and so on.

Interval in ½-tones	*Example*	*Diminished*	*Minor*	*Perfect*	*Major*	*Augmented*
0	c–c			prime		
1	c–c♯					prime
1	c–d♭		2nd			
2	c–d				2nd	
3	c–d♯					2nd
2	c–e♭♭	3rd				
3	c–e♭		3rd			
4	c–e				3rd	
4	c–f♭	4th				
5	c–f			4th		
6	c–f♯					4th
6	c–g♭	5th				
7	c–g			5th		
8	c–g♯					5th
8	c–a♭		6th			
9	c–a				6th	
10	c–a♯					6th
9	c–b♭♭	7th				
10	c–b♭		7th			
11	c–b				7th	
11	c–c♭¹	8ve				
12	c–c¹			8ve		
13	c–c♯¹					8ve

EXERCISES

1. a. Write major seconds up and down from the following notes, then play them on the piano and sing them: ₁C, ₁G, D, A, e, b, f♯¹, c♯², g♯², d♯³, a♯³, e♯⁴, f³, b♭², e♭², a♭¹, d♭¹, g♭, c♭, F♭.

b. Do the same with minor seconds.

c. Do the same with perfect fifths.

d. Do the same with perfect fourths.

e. Do the same with major thirds.

f. Do the same with minor thirds.

2. a. Write major seconds up and down from the following notes, then play them on the piano: c^4, $b\flat^2$, $a\flat^1$, $g\flat$, $F\flat$, $_1A$, B, $c\sharp$, $d\sharp^1$, $e\sharp^2$.

b. Write minor seconds up and down from the following notes, then play them on the piano: g^4, f^3, $e\flat^2$, $d\flat^1$, $c\flat$, D, $_1E$, $F\sharp$, $g\sharp$, $a\sharp^1$.

c. Write perfect fourths up and down from b, B♭, $f\sharp^1$, and f^2, and perfect fifths up and down from f^3, $b\flat^1$, F♯, and b^2. Then play all of them on the piano.

3. a. Do the same as in exercise 1 but with major sixths.

b. Do the same with minor sixths.

c. Do the same with major sevenths.

d. Do the same with minor sevenths.

e. Write major sixths up and down from the notes given in exercise 2a. Then play them on the piano.

f. Write minor sixths up and down from the notes given in exercise 2b. Then play them on the piano.

4. a. Write the following intervals up from d^1, then play them on the piano and sing them: M6, m3, p5, M2, m7, p8, m6, M3, p4, M7, m2.

b. Write the following intervals down from a♭, then play them on the piano and sing them: m2, M7, p4, M3, m6, p8, m7, M2, p5, m3, M6.

b : INVERSION OF INTERVALS

When the lower tone of a simple interval is shifted an octave up across the upper tone, or when the upper tone is shifted an octave down across the lower tone (for example, d–g to d¹–g or d–g to d–G), this shifting is called an *inversion* of the original interval. The patterns of interval inversion are: (1) Perfect intervals invert into perfect ones, major into minor ones and vice versa, and augmented into diminished ones and vice versa. (2) The numerical values of the two intervals will always add up to nine, because the tone common to both intervals is counted in both. For example, a third inverts into a sixth: 3 + 6 = 9.

EXERCISES

1. a. Write the following intervals alternately up and down from b: M6–m3, m7–M2, p5–p4, m3–M6, M2–m7, p4–p5, m6–M3, M7–m2, M3–m6, m2–M7. The first exercise, for example, should be written:

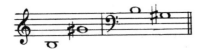

b. Do the same from g♯¹, from e♭², and from A♭.

2. a. Write augmented fourths up and down from the notes given in exercise 1b. Then play them on the piano and sing them.

b. Do the same with diminished fifths.

c. Do the same with augmented seconds.

d. Do the same with diminished sevenths.

3. a. Do the same with augmented fifths.

b. Do the same with diminished fourths.

c. Do the same with augmented sixths.

d. Do the same with diminished thirds.

3

RHYTHM

a : MEASURE, METER, AND METER SIGNATURES

Most musical compositions are subdivided into equal units of time. These units are known as *measures*, and their beginnings and ends are indicated by lines drawn vertically through the staff known as *bars*.†
The subdivision of measures into two, three, or more subunits, or *beats*, is called *meter*. The meter is indicated at the beginning of a piece or wherever a change of meter occurs by a *meter* (or *time*) *signature*, written like a common fraction without the line between the two numbers. The upper number gives the number of beats per measure, and the lower one the note value of each beat. For example, $\frac{3}{4}$ means: three beats per measure, each a quarter-note in length.

EXERCISES

1. Fill one measure of the given meter, using only notes of the beat value:

  a. $\frac{2}{2}, \frac{2}{4}, \frac{2}{8} - \frac{4}{4}, \frac{4}{8}$ c. $\frac{6}{4}, \frac{6}{8}, \frac{6}{16}, \frac{12}{8}, \frac{12}{16}$

  b. $\frac{3}{2}, \frac{3}{4}, \frac{3}{8}, \frac{3}{16} - \frac{9}{8}, \frac{9}{16}$ d. $\frac{5}{4}, \frac{5}{8}, \frac{7}{8}, \frac{7}{16}$

These groups of meters are known respectively as (a) simple *duple* and compound duple, or *quadruple;* (b) simple *triple* and compound triple; (c) mixed

† Colloquially the shorter term "bar" is often used for "measure."

compound or duple compound (6) and quadruple compound (12); and (d) *combination* meters. (In order to avoid the confusing distinction between "compound duple" and "duple compound," many prefer the term "quadruple" to "compound duple.")

2. Fill one measure of the given meter, using only notes of one value as indicated and rests where needed. (For example, the student should write seven measures in $\frac{4}{4}$, the first using only quarter-notes, the second using only eighth-notes cross-beamed in beat groups, the third using a dotted half-note and a quarter-rest, and so on.)

Meter	*Note values*
$\frac{4}{4}$	$\frac{1}{4}$, $\frac{1}{8}$, dotted $\frac{1}{2}$, whole, $\frac{1}{16}$, dotted $\frac{1}{4}$, $\frac{1}{2}$
$\frac{2}{2}$	$\frac{1}{4}$, $\frac{1}{8}$, dotted $\frac{1}{2}$, whole, $\frac{1}{16}$, dotted $\frac{1}{4}$, $\frac{1}{2}$
$\frac{2}{4}$	$\frac{1}{4}$, $\frac{1}{8}$, dotted $\frac{1}{4}$, $\frac{1}{2}$, $\frac{1}{16}$, dotted $\frac{1}{8}$
$\frac{4}{8}$	$\frac{1}{4}$, $\frac{1}{8}$, dotted $\frac{1}{4}$, $\frac{1}{2}$, $\frac{1}{16}$, dotted $\frac{1}{8}$
$\frac{3}{4}$	$\frac{1}{8}$, $\frac{1}{4}$, dotted $\frac{1}{2}$, $\frac{1}{16}$, $\frac{1}{2}$
$\frac{3}{8}$	$\frac{1}{8}$, $\frac{1}{4}$, dotted $\frac{1}{4}$, $\frac{1}{16}$, $\frac{1}{32}$
$\frac{6}{8}$	$\frac{1}{8}$, dotted $\frac{1}{2}$, $\frac{1}{16}$, dotted $\frac{1}{4}$
$\frac{9}{8}$	$\frac{1}{8}$, dotted $\frac{1}{2}$, $\frac{1}{16}$, dotted $\frac{1}{4}$
$\frac{3}{2}$	$\frac{1}{4}$, whole, $\frac{1}{8}$, dotted whole, $\frac{1}{2}$
$\frac{6}{4}$	$\frac{1}{4}$, dotted whole, $\frac{1}{8}$, dotted $\frac{1}{2}$
$\frac{5}{4}$	$\frac{1}{4}$, dotted $\frac{1}{2}$, whole, $\frac{1}{8}$, $\frac{1}{2}$
$\frac{7}{8}$	$\frac{1}{8}$, $\frac{1}{4}$, dotted $\frac{1}{2}$, $\frac{1}{2}$, dotted $\frac{1}{4}$

b : CROSS BEAMS

In compound (including quadruple) and combination meters several beats often form larger subunits, each of which is notationally treated like a single beat. For instance, $\frac{6}{8}$ is always divided $\frac{3}{8} + \frac{3}{8}$. In this meter note values shorter than a dotted half but longer than a dotted quarter must be represented by ties: | ♩. ⁀ ♪♩ | or | ♪♩ ♩ ♪ | .

Similarly, we have to write │♩♩♩ ♪♩│ rather than │♩♩♩ ♩│, since the latter would be interpreted as a $\frac{3}{4}$ meter. Likewise, $\frac{4}{4} = \frac{2}{4} + \frac{2}{4}$, $\frac{6}{4} = \frac{3}{4} + \frac{3}{4}$, $\frac{9}{8} = \frac{3}{8} + \frac{3}{8} + \frac{3}{8}$, and $\frac{12}{8} = \frac{3}{8} + \frac{3}{8} + \frac{3}{8} + \frac{3}{8}$. Wherever possible, these larger subunits are, like the beats of simple meters, made visible with the aid of *beams* that connect all the notes within them.

Usually the start of each subunit or beat is visually defined, that is, it is represented by a note. This note may be longer than the subunit or beat, for example: $\frac{4}{4}$ ♩. ♩│ . On the other hand, when such a longer note starts in the middle of one subunit or beat and continues into the next one, it is often preferable to use a tie rather than a long note value: $\frac{4}{4}$ ♩. ♪♩ ♩│ rather than $\frac{4}{4}$ ♩. ♩. ♩│ . The tie must also be used for holding a note from one measure into the next one.

The directions of partial beams, as well as interruptions in sub-beams, further help to identify the meter, for example: $\frac{6}{8}$ ♫♫♫│ and the same rhythm in a different meter: $\frac{12}{16}$ ♫♫♫│ .

EXERCISES

Use measure bars, ties, and beams to render each of the following passages in these five meters: $\frac{2}{4}$, $\frac{3}{4}$, $\frac{6}{8}$, $\frac{3}{2}$, $\frac{6}{16}$.

1. ♪ ♪♪♪♪♪ ⁊ ♪♪♪ ⁊ ♪ ♪♪♪. ♪♪

2. ♪ ♪. ♪♩ ♪ ⁊ ♪♪ ♪ ⁊· ♪ ♪♪

3. ♪. ♪ ♪♪⁊ ♪♪♪. ♪♪ ⁊ ♪♪⁊ ♪♪

Long note values may be appropriately split into smaller ones tied to each other. The first of these exercises, for example, reads as follows:

c : IRREGULAR DIVISIONS OF BEATS

Any note value may be subdivided. The usual subdivision is by two or four equal values. If a subdivision by three equal values is desired, these three notes are written with the same value as the usual two but with an oblique "3" above or below the group: ♩♩♩ (= ♩♩) . Such a group is called a *triplet*. Similarly when five or six equal notes are wanted in place of the usual four, they are written with the same value as the latter but with a "5" or "6" added: ♫♫♫ = ♫♫♫ ♫♫♫♫ . Such groups are called *quintuplets* and *sixtuplets* (also, quintoles and sixtoles).

EXERCISES

Write a group of four measures in each of the following meters and use in each example all the figures shown; in every case the last measure should have but one or two notes or one note and a rest:

1. $\frac{4}{4}$ ♫ , ♫♫♫ , ♫♫ , ♫♫

2. $\frac{6}{8}$ ♫ , ♫♫♫ , ♫♫

3. $\frac{3}{4}$ ♫ , ♫♫

4. $\frac{3}{2}$ ♫♫♫ , ♩♩♩ , ♫♫♫

5. $\frac{6}{16}$ ♫ , ♫♫♫ , ♫♫

d : STRONG AND WEAK BEATS

The beats of a measure, though mathematically equal, are psychologically differentiated into *strong* and *weak beats* (which must not be equated with loud and soft tones!). In simple meters only the first beat of a measure is heard as strong. In compound and combination meters the first beat of each larger subunit of the measure is also strong. This is known as metric stress. Equally important for our purposes is harmonic stress, meaning that a beat is heard as strong when it introduces a change of harmony. Rhythmic, melodic, contrapuntal, and dynamic stresses are less important in this study.

EXERCISES

1. Write two full measures in each of the following meters, using only notes of beat value. Indicate strong beats by accents (>) and describe each meter by such terms as simple, compound, mixed, combination, duple, triple, and quadruple. When a meter admits of several stress interpretations (combination meters, for example: $\frac{5}{8}$ ♫♩ ♫♫ or ♫♫ ♫♩), write one example of each kind: $\frac{2}{2}, \frac{3}{2}, \frac{2}{4}, \frac{3}{4}, \frac{4}{4}, \frac{5}{4}, \frac{6}{4}, \frac{7}{4}, \frac{2}{8}, \frac{3}{8}, \frac{4}{8}, \frac{5}{8}, \frac{6}{8}, \frac{7}{8}, \frac{8}{8}, \frac{9}{8}, \frac{12}{8}, \frac{3}{16}, \frac{5}{16}, \frac{6}{16}, \frac{7}{16}, \frac{9}{16}, \frac{12}{16}.$

2. Perform all these exercises by tapping all beats with one hand and only the strong beats with the other.

e : RHYTHM IN THE PHRASE AND THE PERIOD

(1) : Rhythm in the Phrase

After the measure the next larger unit in music is the *phrase*, which is comparable to a clause in speech and may be described as "a musical unit that can be sung in one breath." Phrases are of similar, though not of equal, length. A satisfactory phrase, being a unit, obeys certain rules of taste at the beginning, in the middle, and at the end. It may start on a strong beat or on a weak one. In the latter case the first measure of the phrase begins with the first strong beat, and the notes preceding it are called the *upbeat*. (The term "pick-up" is better avoided.) In order to be intelligible and pleasing, a phrase must have a certain regularity. Such regularity is based on *motifs*, which are note groups made recognizable through repetition. The basic ingredient of such motifs is rhythm. At the end of a phrase the rhythm usually slows down and comes to a rest to permit, as it were, the taking of a fresh breath.   Here are two examples:

My Country 'Tis of Thee

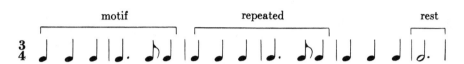

Oh My Darling Clementine

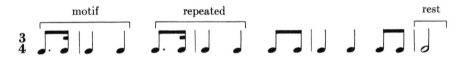

In the following exercises use the same approach; include repeated motifs in each and come to a rest at the end.

EXERCISES

1. a. Write pleasing rhythmic phrases of four to six measures in the following meters using only the given note values, except that the last measure of each phrase should contain only one measure-filling note value.   Rests and ties may be used, but there should be a note on every strong beat.

b. Perform all these phrases by tapping all beats with one hand and only the strong beats with the other.

2. a. Treat the following exercises as in exercise 1a:

b. Perform these exercises as in exercise 1b.

(2) : *Rhythm in the Period*

After the phrase the next larger musical unit is the *period*, comparable
to the sentence in speech. Unlike phrases, periods do not occur in all
music, but they are very common in the music of the past two hundred
years. A period usually consists of two to four phrases. As some
measures within a phrase correspond or are repeated, so are phrases
or motifs repeated within a period to give it coherence. Such correspondences may occur in any conceivable way, but without them no
intelligible order or pattern can be established. Two examples will
clarify this:

Oh Susanna

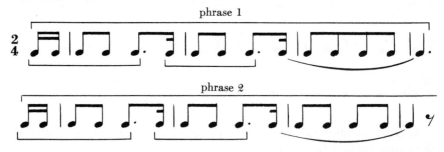

Happy Birthday

In the first example the upbeat motif, despite small changes, remains recognizable throughout; the two phrases are identical in rhythm. In the second example the starting motif is immediately repeated, then slightly changed before its final repetition.

In the following exercises observe rigidly the following procedure:

1. Tap the strong beats with a foot and count them; this gives the number of measures. Then write the correct number of bar lines and observe whether the melody starts on a strong beat or with an upbeat.

2. While continuing to tap the strong beats with the foot, tap all beats with one hand and count how many there are per measure. (Count from one foot-tap to the next, without counting the second foot-tap.) Then write down the meter (or time) signature.

3. Memorize the melody as a whole with the aid of motif and phrase repetitions.

4. Count the tones of the melody in each measure and write the number above each measure.

5. Distribute the tones in each measure among the beats.

EXERCISES

1. Write out the rhythmic plans of the first phrases or periods of the following songs from memory or from dictation, check them against the printed versions (HC† Nos. 2, 5, 69, 59, 27, 13, 8, 9, 120, 114, and 83), and indicate the correspondences in each case as in the preceding examples:

† *Home and Community Song Book,* see p. 5.

   a. "The Star-Spangled Banner" (eight measures)

   b. "America the Beautiful" (eight measures)

   c. "Volga Boatmen" (four measures)

   d. "Londonderry Air" (eight measures)

   e. "Swansea Town" (eight measures)

   f. "Annie Laurie" (eight measures)

   g. "Old Folks at Home" (eight measures)

   h. "My Old Kentucky Home" (eight measures)

   i. "Silent Night" (twelve measures)

   j. "O Come, All Ye Faithful" (eight measures)

   k. "O Isis and Osiris" (twenty measures)

2. Write pleasing periods of seven to eight measures each with the aid of the given motifs and in the indicated meters:

f : IRREGULAR DIVISIONS OF MEASURES AND SYNCOPATION

(1) : *Irregular Divisions of Measures*

Sometimes a part of a measure or an entire measure is irregularly sub-divided so that two beats are replaced by three equally long notes or three beats by two or four equally long notes. Here are some examples which show how the note values of such irregular divisions are written: in $\frac{4}{4}$:| ♩♩♩ ♩♩♩ | ; in $\frac{2}{2}$:| 𝅗𝅥 𝅗𝅥 𝅗𝅥 | and in $\frac{6}{8}$:| ♫♫ ♩♩♩ | . The last of these, unless further subdivided, such as | ♫♫ ♩. ♫ | , may also be written: | ♫♫ ♩.♫ | or | ♫♫ ♩.♩. | . Such irregular divisions are called "duols" or "duplets," "triplets," and "quadruplets."

EXERCISES

Write pleasing eight-measure periods involving the following patterns and the given meters:

(2) : *Syncopation*

Some irregular rhythms can be written with the aid of ties: | ♩. ♪♫ | | ♩. ♪♩ | . In such instances the tied-on off-beat is accented, because it takes over the accent from the tied-on main beat. Such off-beat accentuation is the chief characteristic of a *syncope*, which is the omis-

sion of a main-beat accent and its replacement by one on a weak part
of the measure.   There are various types of syncopation or off-beat
accentuation: [music notation] , [music notation] , and [music notation] .   Often
a syncopated rhythm is established merely by accentuation without
rhythmic irregularity: [music notation] .

EXERCISES

Write two eight-measure periods and include in each several types of syncopation.   Then tap the beats with the foot and the rhythm with the hand.

4

MAJOR AND MINOR

Every advanced civilization achieves a *tone system*, which is a systematic order of all the pitches used in a particular society. Such a system determines the limits of range and the number of pitches in an octave, and then arranges all these pitches in a ladder-like order, which is called a *gamut*. Like any systematic row of tones this may be called a *scale* (from Latin: *scala* = ladder), but this term is usually reserved for a more specific meaning. Today the gamut of Western music has a range of eight octaves, each divided into twelve equal half-tone *intervals*, though some have divided the octave into 24, 36, 48, 53, and even 96 equal intervals. In other periods and civilizations the gamut has extended over as little as two octaves and has contained from five to over twenty unequally spaced pitches per octave.

A gamut is the result of a combination of all the tunes known in a society. Once such a system is achieved, it soon becomes evident that some tunes employ only certain tones of the gamut while others use different selections from it. Such a selection from the gamut is a *genus* (plural *genera*), or a gender, or again a scale. During the Middle Ages, for example, when the Western tone system emerged, musicians generally used a genus of only seven of the twelve tones of the octave and therefore assigned letter names only to these seven tones. These tones, which are the ones represented by the white keys on the piano, form the *diatonic* genus (or scale). Scottish folk songs, on the other hand, usually employ a genus of only five tones, represented by the black keys of the piano and known as the five-tone or *pentatonic* genus. Other common genera are the *chromatic* genus, represented by all tones in the octave and actually identical with our gamut, except in range, and the six-tone or *whole-tone* genus, represented by every other tone in the octave. In addition, some contemporary composers employ genera of eight, nine, and ten tones in the octave, while non-European cultures have used genders with intervals that cannot be reproduced in the Western tone system, such as the five- and seven-tone genders of Java which approach even spacing in the octave.

This second discovery, that of the genera, led to a third one: The tunes within any genus differ further with respect to the order, emphasis, or importance of the pitches. This internal order of the tones of a genus is called *mode*. One type of mode, widely employed throughout the world (for example, by the Hindus and the Arabs), is based on melodic order, each mode being essentially a short melodic formula. In the other type of mode, characteristic of Western music, the order is not one of melody but of emphasis. The pitches may be systematically studied in an ascending or descending scale with the chief tone, the *tonic*, at the start or in the center. Such a mode starts at a definite point in the gamut, follows the interval pattern of a particular genus, and ends an octave above or below the starting point, though it may be repeated in each octave of the gamut.

Western music has employed a variety of modes, but since the seventeenth century two modes have predominated: *Major* and *Minor*. Either consists of seven tones, or *steps*, per octave, which are known by the following names in ascending order:

I   tonic (the emphasized chief pitch)
II   supertonic
III   mediant (middle between the two chief pitches)
IV   subdominant
V   dominant (pitch of secondary emphasis)
VI   submediant
VII   subtonic

The logic of the application of these terms becomes clear from the following arrangement of the steps, which shows that all steps labeled "sub" are as far below the tonic as the corresponding steps are above it:

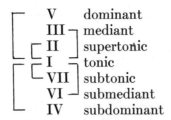

Major and Minor differ in their interval patterns, which are, ascending from the tonic:

Major: whole-tone, whole-tone, half-tone, whole-tone, whole-tone, whole-tone, half-tone

Minor: whole-tone, half-tone, whole-tone, whole-tone, half-tone, whole-tone, whole-tone

These interval patterns are easily remembered as:

Major: 2-½-3-½ (two tones, one half-tone, three tones, one half-tone)

Minor: 1-½-2-½-2 (one tone, one half-tone, two tones, one half-tone, two tones)

Put in another way, the half-tone steps occur in Major between the third and fourth and between the seventh and eighth steps, and in Minor between the second and third and between the fifth and sixth steps.

The names of the two modes are derived from the prevailing type of interval which each contains, counting every interval from the tonic up to each of the following seven tones:

Major: M2–M3–p4–p5–M6–M7–p8 — four major, three perfect intervals

Minor: M2–m3–p4–p5–m6–m7–p8 — one major, three minor, three perfect intervals

This comparison shows that the two modes differ in three steps: III, VI, and VII. All of these form major intervals with the tonic in Major, and minor intervals with the tonic in Minor. This is the reason that the two modes have been named Major and Minor.

b : NOTATION AND KEY SIGNATURES

Any mode may be started on any pitch of a gamut as long as the intervals needed for the modal pattern are available. The process of shifting a modal pattern from one pitch level to another is called *transposition*. In the Western tone system of twelve equal intervals in the octave, any modal pattern may be started on any one of the twelve tones; in other words, every mode may be transposed twelve times. These twelve transpositions are known as the *keys* of the particular mode, each of which is represented by its *scale*. Consequently, there are twelve major and twelve minor keys and scales.

These keys are named after their tonics: for example, C Major and C Minor. Some of the tonics have several enharmonic names, such as C-sharp and D-flat (see Chapter 1, section e); for this reason there are more than twelve keys in notation, although in actual sound there are only twelve of each mode. Two keys, like two notes, are enharmonic when they are different in notation but identical in sound.

Enharmonic notes are a result of the fact that there are only seven letter names for twelve tones, the other names consisting of the same letters with accidentals added. Only the notes that correspond to the seven basic names have their own places in the staff. Both the adoption of the seven letter names and this peculiarity of staff notation result from the establishment of the predominant seven-tone genus in the Middle Ages.

In order to make the notation of scales uniform, each of the seven tone names must occur only once per octave in every scale so that the corresponding notes are evenly and uninterruptedly distributed across

the staff. For example, there is no major or minor scale in which both
B and B-flat or C and C-sharp occur:

but not:

The unwieldiness of the second scale notation is immediately evident
in the disturbing use of two notes in some places and the omission of
notes in others. As long as they have different letter names, consecutive scale steps, whether half-tone or whole-tone steps, are called
diatonic. All our scales are diatonic. On the other hand, different
tones derived from the same basic note through different accidentals,
such as C and C-sharp, are called *chromatic*.

Each of the twelve keys in both modes is characterized by certain
accidentals (or the lack of them). The key in which a piece of music
is to be performed is indicated by a *key signature*, which consists of the
accidentals peculiar to the particular key placed in their appropriate
places on the staff at the beginning of every line of the music, with the
understanding that they are to be applied throughout the piece in all
octaves. Two examples of key signatures are:

and

Conveniently enough, it has been found that in each mode every key
has its particular number and distribution of accidentals, and that no
key signature includes both sharps and flats. The sharps and flats in

key signatures are always written in the following order and spacing in the treble and bass clefs

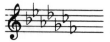

and

EXERCISES

1. Using quarter-notes only, write one octave each, from tonic up to tonic, of eight major scales, starting the first on C and each succeeding one on the dominant (fifth step) of the preceding scale. Complete the transposition by following the whole- and half-tones of the Major pattern and using all needed accidentals. Then write these accidentals as a key signature in a space which has been left at the start of the scale. Indicate all half-steps. For example:

2. Do the same, but start the first scale on c^3 and each succeeding one on the subdominant (fourth step) of the preceding scale, each a fifth lower.

c : CIRCLES OF FIFTHS AND KEY-SIGNATURE
RULES FOR MAJORS

The rules of key signatures that emerge from the preceding exercises are best remembered with the aid of *circles of fifths*. These circles reveal the interesting fact that twelve consecutive fifths include all twelve tones of the octave and then return, in a higher octave, to the pitch of the starting tone:

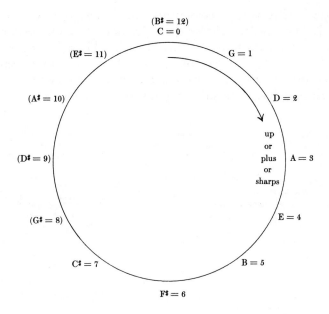

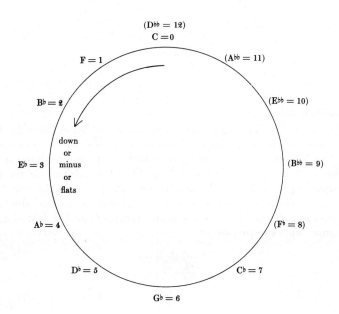

In keys with seven accidentals, all seven steps are sharped or flatted. In those with eight or more accidentals, cumbersome double-sharps or double-flats must be introduced. These keys are therefore used rarely and only in brief passages. They are put in parentheses in the preceding circles and are omitted from the following one, which includes all major keys usually employed in our music.

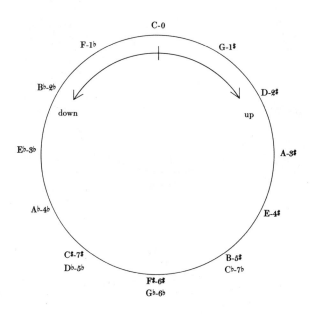

Key-signature rule 1 :

The sharps and flats of key signatures are always written in the order by which they are added when ascending or descending from C in the preceding circle of fifths. In Major, when ascending by a fifth, add the one sharp or subtract the one flat in the key signature which modifies the subtonic of the new key. When descending by a fifth, subtract the one sharp or add the one flat which modifies the subdominant of the new key. Therefore, to find the tonic of a piece written in a major key, go one scale step up from the last sharp of the key signature (for example, in the last sharp is G-sharp, therefore the tonic is A), or go four steps down from the last flat of the key signature (for example, in

the last flat is A-flat, therefore the tonic is E-flat).

Key-signature rule 2 :
The flats and sharps in the key signatures of enharmonic keys always add up to twelve. (For example, B Major has five sharps and C-flat Major has seven flats.)

Key-signature rule 3 :
When ascending from a key to its chromatic neighbor, for instance from C Major to C-sharp Major (but not from C to D-flat, which is a diatonic ascent), add seven accidentals in the key signature (that is, subtract flats and add sharps in the combined amount of seven); when descending chromatically, subtract seven accidentals (that is, subtract sharps and add flats to a total of seven). For example, going from B-flat Major to B Major means going from two flats to five sharps $(2 + 5 = 7)$, and the reverse means going from five sharps to two flats.

Key-signature rule 4 :
When ascending from a key to one a major second higher, add two accidentals in the key signature; when descending by a major second, subtract two accidentals. For example, G Major has one sharp; therefore, A Major has three sharps $(1 + 2)$, and F Major has one flat $(1 - 2 = -1)$.

EXERCISES

1. a. Copy the three circles of fifths.

b. Make a list of the keys of the first two circles in the direction of the arrows, each with its accidentals in correct order. (For example, A: F♯, C♯, G♯)

c. Learn the third circle of fifths by heart.

2. a. Using quarter-notes only, write out one octave each, from tonic down to tonic, of all scales listed in the third circle of fifths in chromatic order with all accidentals and key signatures.

   b. Using quarter-notes only, write out one octave each, from tonic down to tonic, of the following scales: C♭, D♭, E♭, F, G, A, B, C♯; F♯, E, D, C, B♭, A♭, G♭.

3. a. Learn to recite rapidly the fifteen scales, one octave from tonic up to tonic.   The order may be chromatic or around the third circle clockwise (up) from C to C-sharp and then counterclockwise (down) from C to C-flat.

   b. Learn to recite the fifteen scales, one octave from tonic down to tonic.

d : CIRCLES OF FIFTHS AND KEY-SIGNATURE RULES FOR MINORS

The key signatures of the Minors are easily learned by relating them to those of the Majors with one of the three following "rules of three":

1. Shift the zero point in the circles of fifths of Majors by three fifths from "north" to "east" — from C to A:

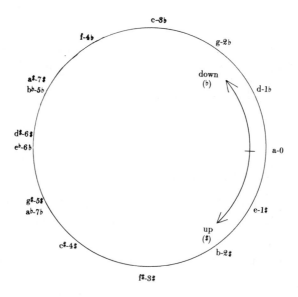

2. Retain the circles of Majors, but subtract from each key signature three accidentals:

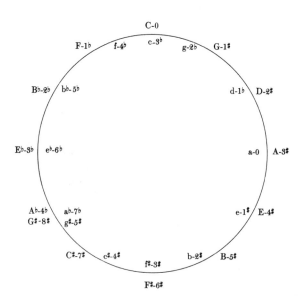

This is the rule of *tonic Majors and Minors*, which are Majors and Minors starting on the same tonic, sometimes also called "parallel Majors and Minors." Any tonic Major and Minor differ by three accidentals, since the third, sixth, and seventh steps differ, being one half-tone higher in Major than in Minor. Therefore, when the key signature of a Major is known, that of the tonic Minor is found by canceling sharps or adding flats totaling three; and similarly, when the key signature of a Minor is known, that of the tonic Major is found by canceling flats or adding sharps totaling three.

3. Retain the circles of Majors but go three scale steps (a minor third) down from the tonic of any Major to obtain the tonic of the Minor with the same key signature. Similarly, ascend three scale steps (a minor third) from the tonic of any Minor to obtain that of the Major with the same key signature. This is the rule of *relative Majors and Minors*, which are Majors and Minors related by the same key signatures and sharing the same notes:

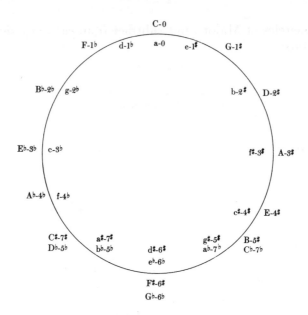

EXERCISES

1. a. Memorize rules 2 and 3 and the two circles of fifths which are included in them.

b. Draw three circles of fifths for Minors similar to those given in section c for Majors — one for ascending fifths, one for descending ones, and one for both combined up to seven sharps and down to seven flats. In all three place A Minor "north." (When symbolizing keys, capital letters by themselves indicate Majors and lower-case letters Minors.)

2. a. Using the rule of tonic Majors and Minors, establish the key signatures of c, a, b, a♭, b♭, g, and d. For example, E Major has four sharps; therefore E Minor has one sharp (4–3).

b. Using the rule of relative Majors and Minors, establish the key signatures of c♯, f, g♯, e♭, f♯, a♯, e, and d♯.

c. Make a list of the Minors as given in the last preceding circle of fifths, up and down from A Minor, each with its accidentals in correct order. (For example, f: B♭, E♭, A♭, D♭)

3. a. Learn to recite rapidly the fifteen Minor scales, one octave up from tonic to tonic. The order may be chromatic or around the last circle of fifths, clockwise to A-sharp Minor and then counterclockwise from A Minor to A-flat Minor.

b. Learn to recite all fifteen Minors, one octave down from tonic to tonic.

e : HARMONIC AND MELODIC MINORS

In section d we studied the *natural* forms of the Minor, which follow the key signatures. Frequently, however, Minors are used in modified forms. The most common of these is the *harmonic* Minor, in which the natural subtonic is replaced by the seventh step of the tonic Major; that is, the natural subtonic is raised by a half-tone in order to obtain a half-tone step between the seventh and eighth steps. This half-tone step is called the *leading tone* because of its strong tendency to "lead up" to the tonic.

The *alteration* of the subtonic in Minor, which raises it by a half-tone, enlarges the major second between the sixth and seventh steps to an augmented second, an interval characteristic of the harmonic Minor. In vocal melodies this augmented second is often avoided because it is hard to sing and has a somewhat foreign, oriental quality. To smooth out this interval, another admixture from the tonic Major has been introduced into the Minor: the major sixth. This mixed mode, which contains both the raised sixth and seventh steps, is called *melodic* Minor. It is especially favored in ascending melodies; descending melodic lines do not need the leading tone and often revert to the natural Minor.

These modifications do not affect the key signature, which remains that of the natural Minor. The raised sixth and seventh steps are indicated by accidentals. The patterns of the three types of Minors are (ascending):

natural: 1–½–2–½–2

harmonic: 1–½–2–½–1½–½

melodic: 1–½–4–½

EXERCISES

1. a. Using quarter-notes only, write out one octave each, from tonic up to tonic, of eight harmonic minor scales, starting on A and continuing by fifths upward. Use all needed accidentals, but also indicate the key signature of each scale. Indicate all steps of minor and augmented seconds, as in the examples above.

b. Do the same, but start on a² and descend by fifths.

c. Make a list of all Minors of the third circle of fifths given in section d with their respective leading tones. (For example, a: G♯)

d. Using quarter-notes only, write out the melodic minor scales (with submediant and subtonic raised on the way up and unaltered, or natural, on the way down) one octave up from the tonic and back, starting with A Minor and continuing through the circle of fifths up to seven sharps, then down to seven flats.

2. a. Write out one octave each, from tonic down to tonic, of the following harmonic Minors: c, d, e, f, and g. Arrange each in a different rhythm within three measures of $\frac{4}{4}$ meter, using only half- and quarter-notes, except for an occasional whole-note in the third measure.

b. Do the same with f♯, g♯, a, b, and c♯, but arrange each within four measures of $\frac{3}{4}$ meter, the last measure being filled by a dotted half-note.

c. Do the same with d♯, e♭, a♯, b♭, and a♭, but arrange each within two measures of $\frac{6}{8}$ meter, using only quarter- and eighth-notes, excepted for a dotted quarter-note in the last half of the second measure.

3. a. Draw a circle of fifths, eight fifths up and down from C, and combine Majors and Minors of the same key signature (relative Majors and Minors).

Write the Majors outside the circle and the Minors inside, opposite the relative Majors.

b. Draw a circle of fifths, eight fifths up and down from C, and combine tonic Majors and Minors, indicating their various key signatures. Write the Majors outside the circle and the Minors inside, opposite the tonic Majors.

f : MAJOR AND MINOR SCALES

Every major and minor scale has seven tones per octave. In order to play seven keys with five fingers, two ideas are applied to the keyboard: (1) The thumb is passed smoothly underneath the other fingers when either hand moves away from the body, and the fingers are passed smoothly over the thumb on the way toward the body. (2) To cover seven keys in each octave, we play twice with fingers 1 (thumb), 2, and 3 in succession and once with finger 4. The fingering is determined, therefore, by where the fourth finger occurs in each scale and hand. This is shown here schematically:

	MAJORS:		
Right hand 4th finger falls on:	*Keys*	*Left hand* 4th finger falls on:	
	Bb	F	
	Bb	Bb	Eb ─
	Bb	Eb	Ab
Bb or A#	Bb	Ab	Db — 4th step
	Bb	Db	Gb ─
	A#	F#	F#
	A#	B	F#
	D#	E	F# ─ F# or Gb
7th step	G#	A	B ─
	C#	D	E
	F#	G	A — 2nd step
	B	C	D
		F	G ─

For example, in A-flat Major the fourth finger of the right hand will be taken on B-flat. Ascending from the B-flat, fingers 1–2–3–1–2–3 will follow, with the fourth finger again falling on B-flat. In the left hand the fourth finger is taken on the fourth step, the D-flat, and, ascending from D-flat, fingers 3–2–1–3–2–1 will follow, with the fourth finger again taken on D-flat. This procedure applies equally to all scales once the place of the fourth finger has been determined.

The fingerings of the Minors may be remembered either in reference to those of the relative and tonic Majors or independently, as shown in the two tables that follow:

HARMONIC MINORS:

Right hand 4th finger falls on:		Keys		Left hand 4th finger falls on:
the same key as in relative Major	Bb	f		the same key as in relative Major
	Bb	bb	Gb	
	Bb	eb	Gb	
	A♯	g♯	C♯	
	D♯	c♯	F♯	
	G♯	f♯	F♯	
the same key as in tonic Major	A♯	b	F♯	the same key as in tonic Major
	D♯	e	F♯	
	G♯	a	B	
	C♯	d	E	
	F♯	g	A	
	B	c	D	
	Bb	f	G	

		Keys		
Bb or A♯	Bb	f		
	Bb	bb	Gb	Gb
	Bb	eb	Gb	
	A♯	g♯	C♯	C♯
2nd step	D♯	c♯	F♯	F♯
	G♯	f♯	F♯	
7th step	A♯	b	F♯	
	D♯	e	F♯	
	G♯	a	B	2nd step
	C♯	d	E	
	F♯	g	A	
	B	c	D	
		f	G	

The following two easy rules will enable the student to retain most scale fingerings: (1) All scales which have tonics on the white keys follow the C Major fingering, except for the right hand in the F scales and left hand in the B scales. (2) In all scales with tonics on the black keys, the thumb takes the first white key after a black key in the right hand on the way up and in the left hand on the way down.

EXERCISES

1. Play two octaves up and down with correct fingering of C, G, D, A, and E Majors and Minors. Play first Major and then Minor with one hand, then repeat them with the other. Play single notes at least at the rate of one per second (metronome speed 60).

2. Play B and F Majors and Minors in the same way.

3. Play F♯ and D♭ Majors and their relative Minors, d♯ (e♭) and b♭; then F♯ and D♭ (C♯) and their tonic Minors, f♯ and c♯, all in the same way.

4. Play A♭, E♭, and B♭ Majors and Minors in the same way.

5

APPENDIX:

TERMINOLOGY, SYMBOLS, BASIC

ACOUSTICS, AND TRANSPOSITION

a : TEMPO, DYNAMICS, AND TONE PRODUCTION

Even though the study of harmony does not deal directly with original composition, the exercises can be made more musical by involving some elements of *expression*. Expression in music, which is the combination of phrasing and interpretation, consists of three chief elements: tempo, dynamics, and tone production. Tempo determines the speed of the beats; dynamics, the loudness of the tones; and tone production, the way in which a tone is attacked, held, and released.

To indicate *tempo*, musicians use actual measurements, which are derived from the *metronome*. This instrument produces from about 40 to about 200 ticks per minute, and a symbol such as $\downarrow$ = 60 means that the music should approximate a speed in which each quarter-note equals one of 60 ticks per minute, or one second. The note values and the numbers change from piece to piece. In addition to such precise indications, which have been increasingly used since the early nineteenth century, there are many tempo terms which indicate the character and speed of a composition in a more general way. Most of these terms are Italian, but today they are often replaced by descriptive words in any other language. They fall into two categories: terms indicating steady speeds and terms indicating changes of tempo. The most frequent Italian tempo markings and their meanings are:

Terms	*Meaning*
1.	
largo, largamente	broad, very slow
lento, grave, adagio (literally, "at ease"), *larghetto*	slow
andante (literally, "walking"), *andantino*	moderately slow
moderato, allegretto	moderately fast
allegro (literally, "cheerful"), *vivace*	fast
presto	very fast (but before 1750 merely "fast")
prestissimo	as fast as possible
2.	
accelerando (abbreviated *accel.*)	increase speed gradually
a piacere (literally "as it pleases")	somewhat free
ritardando, ritenuto (abbreviated *rit., ritard., riten.*)	decrease speed gradually
tempo rubato (literally, "robbed speed")	somewhat free

Some frequent modifiers applied to both tempos and dynamics are the Italian adjectives *molto* (very), *poco* (a little), *più* (more), and *meno* (less).

Graduated *dynamics*, like differentiated tempos and specific tone production, emerged around 1600 in Italy. Consequently, the most commonly used terms and their abbreviations are all Italian. There are, as with tempos, essentially two types of dynamic indications: one type refers to a prevailing level of loudness; the other, to a changing level. The most usual symbols and terms and their meanings are:

Terms	*Symbols*	*Meaning*
1.		
forte	f	loud
fortissimo	ff	very loud

Terms	*Symbols*	*Meaning*
forte-fortissimo	*fff*	extremely loud
mezzo-forte	*mf*	medium loud
mezzo-piano	*mp*	medium soft
piano	*p*	soft
pianissimo	*pp*	very soft
piano-pianissimo	*ppp*	extremely soft
sforzato, sforzando,		
forte-piano	*sf, sfz, fp* (above or be-low a note)	accent

2.

crescendo	*cresc.,* ⟍	increase loudness gradually
diminuendo,		
descrescendo	*dim., decresc.,*	decrease loudness gradually

Tone production includes several terms and symbols which are applied to almost all voices and instruments, as well as many others which occur only with reference to particular instruments. The three most general terms and their symbols and meanings are:

Terms	*Symbols*	*Meaning*
legato	slur above or below note groups	smoothly connected notes, without interruption
staccato	dots above or below notes	short and interrupted notes
portato	both dots and slurs	long but interrupted notes

Other, more restricted, terms are used (a) in connection with stringed instruments usually played with a bow:

pizzicato (symbol: *pizz.*)	string plucked by a finger
spiccato (symbol: *spicc.*)	light bounce of the bow on a string

(b) in connection with stringed instruments, human voices, and the trombone:

portamento (symbol: a straight line connecting two note heads)   connect two tones by sliding quickly through all intermediate pitches

(c) in connection with keyboard instruments and the harp particularly:

glissando (symbol: a straight line connecting two note heads with the word "gliss.")   connect two notes by gliding over all intervening keys or strings

arpeggio (literally, "in the manner of a harp"; symbol: a wavy line in front of a chord)   present the tones of a chord in rapid succession (rather than together), usually from the bottom to the top

b : THE BASIC PROPERTIES OF MUSICAL TONES

Acoustics is the science of sounds. All sounds we hear are psychological reactions, and most of them relate to physical events that can be described in terms of *vibrations,* or a to-and-fro motion of some material body. Such vibrations set up *waves* in the air in the same way that a rock thrown into a pond sets up waves in the water. If these air waves strike our ear with sufficient force, they produce in us, after a very complicated transformation has taken place in the inner ear and the auditory nerve, the phenomenon of sound.

When we picture a series of waves, we usually draw it in the form of a line that alternately rises above a rest position to a crest and then falls below it to a trough:

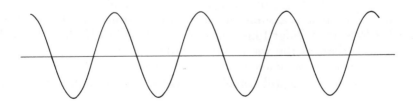

Such a sketch makes clear the three main characteristics of any wave by which it is completely defined:

1. The *wave length*, which is the distance from any point in one wave (such as the crest or the trough) to the corresponding point in the next wave

2. The *amplitude*, or height, of the wave, which is the distance of the crest or the trough from the rest position

3. The *shape*, or contour, of the wave, for most sound waves are not of the simple, smoothly rounded type pictured above, but look something like this:

The first of these characteristics, wave length, is the decisive factor in music; for if the length of the various waves in a series changes or is irregular, we hear a "noise," but if this length remains constant or is regular, we hear a musical tone. Although some noises are used in music (such as the sounds of drums, triangles, and castanets), we shall deal here only with tones.

Each of the three physical characteristics of sound waves may be measured, and these measurements, in turn, are related to our psychological reactions:

1. All sounds, whether noises or tones, travel through the air at the same speed, which varies only with the prevailing air pressure and temperature. Usually this speed is approximately 1100 feet per second. Let us now assume that the waves pictured in the preceding illustrations are regular tone waves of one foot in length. It will be easily seen that, as the wave travels 1100 feet through the air in one second, it will repeat itself 1100 times. If the wave length were two feet, the wave would still travel 1100 feet in one second, but it would

repeat itself only 550 times to cover that distance. The number of waves per second (1100 in the first instance and 550 in the second) is called the *frequency* of the wave. The frequency, in turn, has a psychological correlate: the *pitch*. A frequency of about 262, for example, is heard as middle C. The human ear can hear, or react with the sensation of pitch to, frequencies from about 15 to about 25,000 per second, but on the piano, which represents the most usable musical pitch range, the frequencies vary only from about $27\frac{1}{2}$ to 4185. The shorter the wave, the higher is the frequency and the pitch.

2. The amplitude of a wave depends on the energy or force with which the generating body vibrates and succeeds in agitating the air. This physical energy is measured in units called "ergs" and is related to the psychological response of *loudness*. Differences in the physical energy generated and in the loudness heard, however, are by no means identical. For example, when a tone is played on one violin and then with the same strength on ten violins, the physical energy increases tenfold, but our response in terms of loudness grows only twofold. Because the loudness of a tone is more important to us than the physical energy involved, we are not as interested in the "erg" as in the units used to measure loudness: the *bel* and the *decibel*, which is one tenth of a bel.

3. The different shapes of musical tone waves have been found to yield to a geometric analysis, and this analysis has shown that all but the smoothly rounded waves are composed of several waves in addition to the main wave. The lengths of these additional waves are simple partials (such as $\frac{1}{2}$, $\frac{1}{3}$, $\frac{1}{4}$, or $\frac{1}{5}$) of the length of the main wave, or, what is the same, their frequencies are multiples of that of the main wave (such as 2, 3, 4, or 5 times its frequency). Each of the subwaves corresponds to another pitch, and each musical tone, with few exceptions, is thus composed of several tones called *partials*, which are also known as *fundamental* (the wave length of lowest frequency) and *overtones*. Such a composite tone is called a *klang*. The various wave shapes relate to the different *timbres* or *tone colors*, that is, to the characteristic sounds of the various instruments and voices.

In summary, the waves of musical tones have three physical properties, which are mathematically represented in the following terms and correspond to the following psychological responses:

Wave characteristic	*Mathematical term*	*Psychological response*
length	frequency (waves per second)	pitch
amplitude	energy (erg)	loudness (decibels)
shape	partials (each of which is measurable in terms of frequency and energy)	timbre

Duration is often mentioned as a fourth basic property of tones. However, this factor is not a characteristic of the single wave and is a general ingredient of all our experiences, not only of musical tones.

c : PARTIALS AND FREQUENCY RATIOS OF INTERVALS

The partials that combine in a klang can always be predicted if one knows the fundamental, which is the tone actually heard. As stated in the preceding section, the overtones correspond to multiples of the frequency of the fundamental. This means that, if the frequency of the fundamental (or first partial) is 100 waves per second, the frequency of the first overtone (or second partial) is 200, that of the second overtone (or third partial) is 300, and so on. Or, if the first partial (fundamental) has the frequency of 70, then the second partial (first overtone) has the frequency of 140 (2 × 70), the third partial (second overtone) 210 (3 × 70), and so on.

When the fundamental is C, this series of multiple frequencies corresponds to the following series of notes:

Similarly, when the fundamental is **E**, the series corresponds to the following:

In other words, the series of partials, expressed in intervals, consists of:

1. the fundamental
2. its 8ve
3. 8ve + 5th
4. double 8ve
5. double 8ve + M3
6. double 8ve + 5th
7. double 8ve + m7
8. triple 8ve

9. triple 8ve + M2
10. triple 8ve + M3
11. triple 8ve + a4
12. triple 8ve + 5th
13. triple 8ve + M6
14. triple 8ve + m7
15. triple 8ve + M7
16. quadruple 8ve

   This series continues into infinity, with the intervals becoming progressively smaller. The farther one carries the series, the less important are the partials for the timbre of the tone. The first sixteen partials are, however, fundamental to our musical system in that they present us with eleven of its twelve intervals, although in practice most of the intervals have to be slightly modified (see section d). Nevertheless, these sixteen partials also include four tones that do not belong to our system: partials 7, 11, 13, and 14. These are therefore symbolized differently (by black notes) in the preceding examples. Using the order numbers (1 to 16) in the preceding table of partials, the eleven intervals are obtained between the following pairs of partials respectively:

Interval	*Partials*
minor second	15/16
major second	8/9 or 9/10†

† The existence of two sizes of whole tones and minor sevenths is one of the reasons for the needed modification of intervals.

Interval	*Partials*
minor third	5/6
major third	4/5
fourth	3/4
fifth	2/3
minor sixth	5/8
major sixth	3/5
minor seventh	5/9 or 9/16†
major seventh	8/15
octave	1/2

It will be seen that the order numbers of the partials correspond to the numbers by which the fundamental frequency must be multiplied in each case. All the intervals which nature offers to our ear in a single klang can thus be easily translated into frequency ratios.

From the above series of the first sixteen partials we can, in fact, derive the approximate frequencies of all the tones on the piano, once the frequency of any tone is given. To find the frequency of any tone *above* the given pitch, (1) establish the interval between the two tones, (2) find from the preceding table the order numbers of the two partials that form this interval, (3) place the higher number in the form of a fraction above the lower one, and (4) multiply the given frequency by this fraction. To find the frequency of a tone *below* the given pitch, proceed identically, but place the higher number under the lower one. For example:

1. What is the approximate frequency of $c\sharp^2$ if $a^1 = 440$?
   a. This is an ascending major third.
   b. The order numbers for a major third from the table are 4 and 5.
   c. The fraction is therefore $\frac{5}{4}$.
   d. The approximate frequency of $c\sharp^2$ is therefore $440 \times \frac{5}{4}$, which equals 550.

2. What is the approximate frequency of f^1?
   a. This is a descending major third.
   b. The order numbers are again 4 and 5.

† The existence of two sizes of whole tones and minor sevenths is one of the reasons for the needed modification of intervals.

c. Now the fraction is $\frac{4}{5}$.

d. The approximate frequency of f¹ is therefore $440 \times \frac{4}{5}$, which equals 352.

Only the tritone (the augmented fourth, or diminished fifth) is missing from the first sixteen partials, but it can be easily figured out by adding a minor second to a fourth or by subtracting a minor second from a fifth. Such addition of intervals is done by multiplying the fractions that represent the two intervals — in this case, $\frac{16}{15} \times \frac{4}{3} = \frac{64}{45}$. Subtraction of intervals is achieved by a division of the two fractions, which means that the one representing the interval to be subtracted is inverted, and then the two fractions are multiplied — in this case, $\frac{3}{2} \times \frac{15}{16} = \frac{45}{32}$. The difference between the two fractions for the tritone, $\frac{64}{45}$ and $\frac{45}{32}$, is another reason for modifying the natural intervals in our tone system.

EXERCISES

1. In section b the frequencies of the middle C and of the highest and lowest tones on the piano were mentioned. Derive all three from a¹ = 440.

2. Establish the frequencies of all thirteen tones of the octave a–a¹.

3. Establish the frequencies of the seventh, eleventh, thirteenth, and fourteenth partials of A and bring them by octave transposition to within the octave a–a¹. Compare the frequencies thus obtained with those obtained in exercise 2.

d : EQUAL TEMPERAMENT

The system of partials poses several problems for the musician. To begin with, three intervals appear in two sizes: the major second, the minor seventh, and the tritone. Furthermore, there are partials which fall between the twelve pitches that we recognize in our octave: the seventh, eleventh, thirteenth, and fourteenth partials, as well as many others above the sixteenth. Finally, a most uncomfortable discrepancy emerges when we try to establish the full range of our musical tones: when we tune a piano first in ascending pure octaves, using the ratio $\frac{2}{1}$ up from the lowest C, and then in ascending pure fifths, using the ratio $\frac{3}{2}$ up from the same tone, the resulting pitches for the highest C on the piano, which should be identical, turn out to be different.

EXERCISE

From the middle C (c^1) established in exercise 1 of section c, figure out the frequency of the lowest C on the piano ($_1$C).   Then establish the frequency of c^5, first as the seventh octave of $_1$C and then as the twelfth fifth of $_1$C.

Western music has dealt radically with the partials which fall between the twelve tones of an octave by excluding the problematic intervals from its system.   But the other problems have not been solved so easily.   For example, both wind and string instruments, which deal constantly with pure octaves and fifths, have to compromise whenever they play with a keyboard instrument.

These difficulties have been known since the days of classical Greece.   A number of limited solutions were proposed during the Middle Ages and afterwards, but they were discarded after the one which is used today was found in the eighteenth century.   It is called *equal temperament,* and it is applied to all instruments with more or less fixed pitches, particularly the keyboard instruments.   Equal temperament gives to each of the twelve half-tones of the octave an exactly identical size: to go up by a half-tone, the frequency of the lower pitch must be multiplied by almost 1.06 (more accurately, by 1.059463).

A comparison of the frequencies of the tones in the octave a–a^1 obtained in exercise 2 of section c by using *just* (natural) *intonation* and the frequencies of these tones as found in equal temperament shows their characteristic differences:

	Just intonation	*Equal temperament*
a	220	220
b♭	234.67	233.08

	Just intonation	*Equal temperament*
b	244.44 or 247.5	246.94
c¹	264	261.62
c#¹	275	277.18
d¹	293.33	293.67
eb¹	309.38 or 312.89	311.13
e¹	330	329.63
f¹	352	349.23
f#¹	366.67	369.99
g¹	391.11 or 396	391.99
g#¹	412.5	415.3
a¹	440	440

Thus in equal temperament and just intonation all intervals except the octave differ:

The following equal-tempered intervals are slightly larger: M3, 4th, M6, M7.

The following equal-tempered intervals are slightly smaller: m2, m3, 5th, m6.

The following equal-tempered intervals are compromises between the two values obtained for them in just intonation: M2, tritone, m7.

In general, major intervals are larger in equal temperament than in just intonation, and minor intervals are smaller. Sharps are taken higher and flats taken lower in equal temperament than they would be in just intonation, resulting in an acceptable compromise, which in each case makes a single pitch serve as both a flat and a sharp, where in the past two different pitches had been needed.

e : TRANSPOSITION

The shifting of a melody or of an entire piece of music from one pitch level to another is called *transposition*. When music is transposed, every note in the original setting is shifted by the same interval, this interval being the distance between the original pitch and the pitch desired. Perhaps the simplest way to transpose is to decide upon the first note or notes on the new pitch level, determine the new key signature, and then proceed to read the remainder by consecutive intervals: a third up, two seconds down, a fourth up, and so on.

Another method of transposing is to read the notes in a different clef and add the appropriate key signature. For example, to transpose the following passage a third up, you only have to change to the bass clef and add either three flats or four sharps, playing two octaves higher, of course:

Similarly, transposition by a second up in the treble clef is achieved by reading in the alto clef an octave higher:

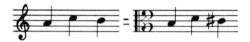

Transposing a second down in the treble clef is achieved by reading in the tenor clef an octave higher:

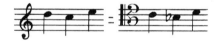

Transposing in the bass clef a third down is easy when reading in the treble clef two octaves lower:

Transposing a second down in the bass clef may be done by reading in the alto clef an octave lower:

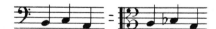

Reading in the tenor clef transposes a fifth up from the bass clef:

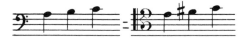

EXERCISES

1. Write the first phrases of three of the songs cited in exercise 1 in Chapter 3, section e(2), in the treble clef and ascribe to each interval its name.

2. Write these phrases one whole-tone higher by establishing each note in two ways:

    a. Transpose each note.

    b. Transpose the first note and then each melodic interval.

Add the correct key signature to each phrase.

3. Do the same:

    a. a half-tone higher   **d.** a minor third lower

    b. a whole-tone lower   **e.** a major third lower

    c. a half-tone lower

4. Play the original phrases on the piano. Then replace the treble clef consecutively by:

    a. the bass clef, while adding first one then another appropriate key signature to effect a transposition by a major and then by a minor third

    b. the alto clef, similarly in two versions — transposing by a major and a minor second up

    c. the tenor clef, again in two versions — transposing by a major and a minor second down

5. Write the original phrases in the bass clef and play them on the piano. Then replace the bass clef (each time in two different key-signature versions as in exercise 4) successively by:

    a. the treble clef   **b.** the alto clef   **c.** the tenor clef

II

DIATONIC HARMONY

6

PRIMARY TRIADS

a : TRIADS

(1) : Types of Triads

A *chord* is the simultaneous combination of three or more different tones, not counting octave duplications. (Two simultaneous tones are referred to as either a harmonic interval or an incomplete chord.) A *harmony* is a chord that is recognized as belonging to a certain key. (Therefore, the study of "harmony" refers to the succession of such harmonies and the relationships among them.) The most frequent type of harmony is the *triad*, which is composed of three tones which are thirds apart from each other, following the pattern 1–3–5, 2–4–6, and so on, with reference to the steps within a particular key. These three tones are called the *root*, the *third*, and the *fifth* of the chord.

Since the major and minor modes contain only major and minor thirds, there are only four types of triads which are possible in these modes:

```
p5
    (m3)
M3          — major triad:
    (M3)
r
```

p5
   (M3)
m3   — *minor* triad:
   (m3)
r

a5
   (M3)
M3   — *augmented* triad:
   (M3)
r

d5
   (m3)
m3   — *diminished* triad:
   (m3)
r

Any step of a major or minor key can be used as the root of a triad, which is then named according to the step of the key which is its root. The following triad, for instance, is derived from C Major and built on the first step of that scale:

It is therefore designated as C I and spoken of as "C one," or as the "tonic triad of C Major." Similarly, the following chord is known as C V and referred to as "C five," or as the "dominant triad of C Major":

This chord may also be read as G I, while the one which we called C I may also represent F V. In general, any chord may belong to several keys, and the key to which it belongs in a given instance can only be determined by the context.

To symbolize the four types of triads, this text employs capital Roman numerals for major triads and small Roman numerals for minor triads, regardless of whether or not these harmonies occur in a major or minor key, as follows:

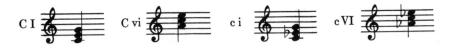

The augmented and diminished triads are symbolized as follows:

Thus the capital numeral actually indicates the major third, the small numeral the minor third; the "+" refers to the augmented fifth, and the "°" (which for better visibility in the staff replaces the "−") to the diminished fifth.

EXERCISES

1. Write the following tonic triads in the form root-third-fifth with their roots on the indicated notes (capital letters indicate major keys; lower-case letters, minor keys):

A–a[1] (meaning: A-Major triad with root on a[1])	F–f[3]	d–d
	g–G	E–e[3]
b–₁B	Ab–ab[1]	f♯–F♯
Db–db[2]	bb–Bb	
eb–eb	C–c[2]	

2. Similarly treat:

F♯–f♯[1]	ab–Ab	f–f[3]	Cb–cb
e–₁E	Gb–gb[1]	Eb–Eb	C♯–c♯[3]
D–d[2]	g♯–₁G♯	c♯–c♯[1]	d♯–D♯
c–c	a♯–a♯[2]	B–₁B	
Bb–bb[3]	G–g	a–a[2]	

3. a. Play a C Major triad with the fingering as shown.   Then transpose it by ascending half-tones through an octave, first with one hand, then with the other:

b. Do the same with an A Minor triad.   The fingering is the same.

4. a. Play a major triad in arpeggio with alternating hands as in the following example.   Then transpose it by ascending half-tones through an octave:

b. Do the same with a minor triad.

(2) : Distribution of Parts

During the late fifteenth century music began to be written in four voice parts, later named, from top to bottom, soprano, alto, tenor, and bass.   Four-part writing, such as that of church hymns, has ever since been regarded as combining the greatest harmonic clarity with a satisfactory fullness of sound.

In a four-part setting one tone of the triad must be doubled.   The best doubling has been found to be that of the root; the next best, that of the fifth.   The doubled third, on the other hand, is pleasant only under certain circumstances.   We shall at first use only the doubling of the root, which may occur in unison between tenor and bass, or at the distance of one, two, or three octaves in any of the three upper parts.

Apart from doublings, the following things determine the character of a triad's sound: (1) the position of the soprano, or the tone of the triad which is heard as the melody tone, and (2) the spacing of parts, or the arrangement of the middle parts (alto and tenor).   Any one of the triad tones may be in the soprano: the octave of the root, the third, or the fifth. Accordingly, we speak of triads in the *position* of the octave, third, or fifth, and these positions may be indicated by the figures 8, 3, or 5 written underneath the bass note. On the other hand, while there are terms for the various arrangements of the middle parts, which concern the distances between the alto and soprano and the alto and tenor (but not between the tenor and bass), there are no symbols to indicate them. When there is room for one or more tones of the triad between alto and soprano and between alto and tenor, the chord is in *open harmony;* when there is no such room in either interval, the chord is in *close harmony;* and when one interval can accommodate another triad tone while the other cannot, the chord is in *mixed harmony.* For example:

Close harmony	*Open harmony*
Pos. of 8ve:	Pos. of 8ve:

Pos. of 3rd: Pos. of 3rd:

Pos. of 5th: Pos. of 5th:

Mixed harmony is possible only when the fifth or the third is doubled:

Pos. of 3rd, mixed har.   Pos. of 5th, mixed har.

A triad in mixed harmony with an octave between alto and soprano or between alto and tenor sounds rather thin, as does a triad in which either of these intervals is larger than an octave, that is, a triad in *extra-wide harmony*. Both these arrangements of middle parts should therefore be avoided.

EXERCISES

Construct alternately major and minor triads on the following tones as roots and write each in all the six versions shown under "close" and "open harmony": f, g², ₁A, b¹, C♯, e♭, G♯, c♭², ₁D♭, d♯¹, E, f♯, a♯¹, B♭, d.

b : I-IV AND I-V PROGRESSIONS

(1) : *Strict Connections*

Movement is essential to music. In the study of harmony, therefore, the movement from one chord to the next is of primary interest. In general, there are three ways in which two parts, or voices, may move relative to each other: (1) When two voices move in the same direction, they are said to be in *similar motion*. A special case of similar motion is *parallel motion*, in which both parts move by the same interval or, what is the same, begin and end the same distance apart. (2) When the two voices move in opposite directions, they are said to be in *contrary motion*. (3) When one voice moves while the other remains on the same pitch, they are said to be in *oblique motion;* here repeating a tone and skipping by an octave are considered identical with holding the same pitch. These motions are illustrated in the following example:

J. S. Bach — *Ermuntre dich* (Melody No. 12 in BR†)

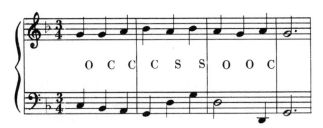

(The abbreviations are: C = contrary, O = oblique, S = similar.)

A chord can be repeated, or it can move to another chord. When it is repeated, the various voices may change their places and skip about without limitation: this is known as *changing the position* of a chord. In moving from one harmony to another, on the other hand, it has been found necessary to avoid unpleasant effects by observing certain *rules of voice leading*. These rules fall mainly into two classes: (1) avoiding the overstressing of any part by reinforcing it with another

† Bach-Riemenschneider, see p. 5.

part, which thereby loses its own melodic independence; and (2) avoiding unmelodic or hard-to-sing intervals in each voice.

Both types of rules are based on the experience of sixteenth-century composers, whose polyphonic, or many-voiced, style of writing was particularly suited to vocal performance. When in the seventeenth and eighteenth centuries independent instrumental music began to rival vocal music, the second class of rules was strongly modified and, in instrumental music, completely abandoned. Since the latter part of the nineteenth century the first class has also been greatly modified, if not abandoned. We shall begin this study with a strict observance of the rules as they were followed in vocal compositions about the middle of the eighteenth century. The style of that period is the basis of all the later developments which will be studied subsequently.

The first rule observed in the connection of chords falls under the first class of voice-leading rules. Since parallel motion is heard as a temporary abandonment of melodic independence, and since parallel primes, fifths, and octaves are heard as reinforcements of tones, it is necessary to follow

Rule 1 :

Avoid parallel (also called consecutive, or open) primes, fifths, and octaves in any two parts.

In order to observe this rule, it is necessary to follow certain procedures when connecting tonic and dominant or tonic and subdominant triads. Such progressions, in which the roots of the two harmonies are a fourth (or fifth) apart, are called *root progressions by fourths.* In these, the two harmonies will always have one tone in common. For achieving root progressions by fourths according to rule 1, it is best to follow the strict

Procedure 1 :

    a. Write the root progression in the bass.
    b. Complete the first chord.
    c. Find the common tone and hold it in the same voice.
    d. Lead the remaining voices stepwise to the nearest tones of the second chord.
    e. If the fifth of the first chord is the common tone and is doubled, hold it in one part only and lead it to the nearest needed chord tone in the other.

Example:

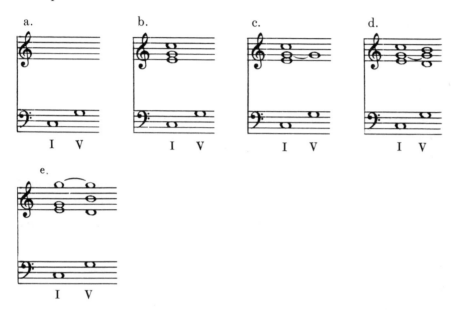

Note that the dominant triad is the same in Minor and Major, since it is derived from the harmonic scale in Minor. The major third, which characterizes every dominant chord, will be indicated in exercises in Minor by the appropriate accidental underneath the bass. In both Major and Minor this third is called the *leading tone*, because it is heard as leading to the tonic. This fact is expressed in

Rule 2 :

The leading tone must be led to the tonic, especially in the soprano, and must never be doubled, for this would bring about parallel primes or octaves.

The use of this rule avoids an unmelodic, frustrating progression which would thwart the expectation aroused by the leading tone.

In the following exercises, and throughout this study, observe

Rule 3 :

When writing for four parts mostly in open harmony, place the soprano in the

treble staff with stems up, the alto in the treble staff with stems down, the tenor in the bass staff with stems up, and the bass in the bass staff with stems down.   When writing mostly in close harmony, place soprano as before, put alto and tenor on a common downward stem in the treble staff, and the bass with stems up or down in the bass staff.

EXERCISES

1. a. Write the following tonic triads in four parts in all positions shown under close and open harmony in section a(2) of this chapter, and lead each chord strictly to its respective dominant triad: G, g, D, d, A, a, C, c, F, f, B♭, b♭. Use proper key signatures, but write all accidentals also in each chord.   Employ half-notes throughout and place the proper accidental for the dominant chord in Minor and the figures I, i, and V underneath the bass.

b. Do the same as in exercise a, but start with the dominant triads and lead them to their respective tonic triads.

2. Write the progressions I–V–I and I–IV–I in the following keys, starting in the position indicated:

    a. position of 3rd, close harmony —E, e

    b. position of 5th, close hamony—B, b

    c. position of 8ve, close harmony — F♯, f♯

    d. position of 3rd, open harmony — C♯, c♯

    e. position of 5th, open harmony —E♭, e♭

    f. position of 8ve, open harmony — A♭, a♭

    g. position of 3rd, close harmony — D♭

    h. position of 5th, open harmony — G♭

    i. position of 8ve, close harmony — C♭

    j. position of 3rd, open harmony — a♯

    k. position of 5th, close harmony — d♯

    l. position of 8ve, open harmony — g♯

3. Play on the piano all the progressions written in the preceding exercises.

4. In accompanying folk songs, marches, waltzes, and other simple melodies, the pianist's left hand will often play the simple triads, disregarding the smooth progressions characteristic of vocal music. Doublings of the third will still be avoided. The chords will normally enter only on main beats and will usually include the melody tone heard at that moment. Three simple variants of such accompaniments are shown here.

Block chords:

March or dance basses:

Broken chords, also called Alberti basses:

Use each of these three types of accompaniment with each of the following examples.† The places where new harmonies *must* enter are marked "*." Occasionally new harmonies may be used to support melody notes other than those marked.

　　a. *Eastern Monarchs, Sages Three* (medieval carol)

† From *Noels* by Marx and Anne Oberndorfer (Chicago: H. T. Fitzsimons Company, 1932).

b. *In dulci jubilo* (medieval carol)

c. *The Babe in Bethlem's Manger* (English carol)

(2) : Free Connections

In order to construct pleasing melodies, it is often necessary to depart
from the strict rules and use *free connections*.   In such connections of
I and V the leading tone, when in a middle part, may occasionally be
led to a tone other than the tonic so that a complete triad may be
obtained, particularly when the next higher voice takes over the
resolution of the leading tone:

In free connections the doubling of the fifth is always good, and at times the third may be doubled. A free connection may also result in an *incomplete triad*. Such a chord must always contain the third in order to indicate whether a major or a minor triad is intended. The fifth is the only tone of a triad that may be omitted. An incomplete triad therefore usually consists of three roots and a third:

EXERCISES

1. a. Supply the middle parts to the following free connections of I and V, add the letter symbol for the key in each exercise, and use the appropriate figures I, i, and V beneath the bass. Find two solutions for each exercise.

b. Supply the middle parts to the following free connections of I and IV, add the letter symbol for the key in each exercise, and use the appropriate figures I, i, IV, and iv beneath the bass.   Find two solutions for each exercise.

c. Play on the piano all the exercises given in a and b.

2. Set out *strictly* the following exercises in four parts, heeding these suggestions:

Suggestion 1 :
Make the melody as interesting as possible by avoiding too many repeated tones in it, especially when going from a weak beat to the succeeding strong one.

Suggestion 2 :
When the same harmony is used twice in succession, this pause in harmonic movement is to be used for melodic movement in the soprano by changing its position (and where necessary that of the other parts also).

The rhythm indicated in the exercises is that of the soprano; the rhythm of the bass and the other parts need not be identical with it. In fact, the holding of common tones helps stress the independence of parts and is very pleasing, as in the following example:

Use correct key signatures and the necessary accidentals for the dominant triads in Minor. These accidentals, which always apply to the third of the chord, are indicated after the Roman numerals. Dashes after such numerals mean the continuation of a harmony under a new soprano note.

a. Begin in close harmony:

C 2/2

I₃   IV   I   –   V   –   I

b. Begin in open harmony:

d 3/4

i₅   V♯   –   i   iv   i   –   V♯   I

c. Begin in close harmony:

E 4/8

V₃   I   –   V   I   V   I   –   IV   –   I

d. Begin in close harmony:

f♯ 3/2

iv₅   –   i   –   V♯   –   i   –   iv   i

e. Begin in open harmony:

I₈ V I   IV I V I   V   I IV – I   V   I – V I

f. Begin in close harmony:

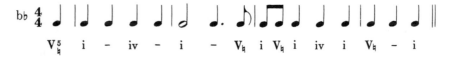

V⁵♮ i – iv – i – V♮ i V♮ i iv i V♮ – i

g. Begin in close harmony:

I₈ V I – IV I IV – I V I IV I V   I IV I V I

h. Begin in open harmony:

d♯ 2/4 🎵

i₃   V×   i   iv   i   V×   i

i. Begin in open harmony:

V₈ – I – V I – IV   I – V I IV I V   I

j. Begin in close harmony:

g 3/4 🎵

iv₃   i   iv   i   V♯   i   iv   i   V♯   i

k. Begin in open harmony:

I₅ IV I - V I - IV - I V I

l. Begin in open harmony:

i₃ V♯ i iv i - V♯ i iv i V♯ - i iv - i V♯ - i V♯ i

c : IV-V PROGRESSIONS

(1) : Strict Connections

Having studied root progressions by fourths, we now turn to *stepwise
root progressions*, or root progressions by seconds, which involve the
connection of triads with roots that are a step apart. In such progressions the two chords contain no common tones. Therefore, in
order to observe rule 1 (see section b(1) of this chapter), one follows
the strict

Procedure 2 :
    a. Write the root progression in the bass.
    b. Complete the first chord.
    *c. Lead all other voices to the nearest tones of the second chord in contrary
motion to the bass.*

Here one of the three upper parts will skip while the others go stepwise.
An example of procedure 2:

Stepwise root progressions are less vigorous than root progressions by fourths, and ascending progressions by seconds are stronger than descending ones. By "strong" and "weak" progressions we do not mean "good" and "bad" ones. Rather, strong progressions are the kind that usually prevail in military marches or gay songs, while weak progressions tend to prevail in melancholy, sad music. (Besides root progressions by fourths and by seconds there are only those by thirds, to be studied later, for progressions by fifths, sevenths, and sixths are identical with these three classes respectively.)

EXERCISES

1. a. Write the subdominant triads of the following keys in all positions shown under open and close harmony in section a(1) and lead each chord to its respective dominant triad. Use figures IV, iv, and V in all exercises and the appropriate accidentals with V in Minor: C, c, G, g, D, d, A, a, E, e, F, f, B♭, b♭.

    b. In the same manner write the dominant triads of the following keys and lead them to their respective subdominant triads: B, b, F♯, f♯, C♯, c♯, E♭, e♭, A♭, a♭, D♭, G♭, C♭, g♯, d♯, a♯.

    c. Play on the piano all the exercises given under a and b.

2. a. Write strict three-chord sequences IV–V–IV in the following keys:
    (1) E♭, starting in position of 3rd, close harmony
    (2) b♭, starting in position of 5th, close harmony
    (3) F, starting in position of 8ve, close harmony
    (4) c, starting in position of 3rd, open harmony
    (5) G, starting in position of 5th, open harmony
    (6) d, starting in position of 8ve, open harmony

b. Write strict three-chord progressions V–IV–V in the following keys, using by turn the various starting arrangements given in exercise 2a: A, e, B, c♯, A♭, g♯.

c. Play on the piano all the exercises given under a and b.

(2) : *Free Connections*

As with root progressions by fourths, free connections may also be used with stepwise root progressions in order to create a more interesting melody. Such free connections often demand doublings other than that of the root, and not all of these other possible doublings are satisfactory. For example, doubling the fifth of IV is always difficult to manage when V follows; and the third of V is the leading tone, which can never be doubled, because such a doubling would result in parallel octaves. These free connections usually include some rather awkward, large skips which seem to invite *crossings in passing* of the sort that occurs when the soprano moves to a tone lower than the preceding alto tone. Such voice leading should be avoided, because it makes it difficult for the ear to follow each part clearly.

Avoid: C   IV   V   Better: C   IV   V

Because of the various complications, use these free connections sparingly at the beginning.

The following exercises represent the few free connections between IV and V that are possible if we want to observe rules 1 and 2 (the avoidance of parallel fifths and octaves, and the resolution of the leading tone to the tonic).

EXERCISES

Write each of the following exercises in two different keys and play each on the piano in at least three different keys:

(Exercises 1 and 2 are best done by using an incomplete IV with tripled root
and a third.   Numbers 3 and 4 are good only in Major, because in Minor an
awkward augmented second would occur in the soprano.   In number 4 the
student may disregard rule 2, because the smooth melodic motion of the
soprano takes the edge off the unfulfilled tendency of the leading tone.   In
numbers 5 through 8 either the third of IV or the fifth of V must be doubled.)

7

APPROACHES TO MELODY (1)

a : STRICT, UNSTRESSED NONHARMONIC TONES

To be satisfactory, a melody must be independent not only with respect to its pitch movement, or *melos*, but also with respect to its rhythm. Up to this point, rhythmic independence has only been possible by changing the position within a chord, which results in melodic skips, or by holding common tones. Yet melody is predominantly stepwise, especially vocal melody. To create stepwise melodies with rhythmic independence, *nonharmonic tones* are often introduced between the chord tones which constitute the soprano (or the other voices). Such nonharmonic tones are always *neighboring tones*, that is, they are always heard as neighbors of a chord tone, forming with it an interval of either a prime or a second. This fact is fundamental to their understanding and application.

We shall use at first only three types of nonharmonic tones, all *unstressed*, that is, occurring between beats or on weak beats. The main beats will continue to carry chord tones only. The first type of nonharmonic tone is called the *passing tone* (p). A passing tone moves stepwise and fills the interval between one chord tone and another. For example:

As seen in the preceding example:

1. There are ascending as well as descending passing tones.

2. The two chord tones between which the passing tone or tones occur need not belong to the same harmony.

3. There may be two passing tones in a row.

The first two statements also apply to the other two types of non-harmonic tones to be studied here. The second class of these is the *turning tone* (t), which stands between two chord tones of the same pitch. These chord tones may or may not belong to the same harmony (as in measures 1 and 2 respectively of the following example):

Measure 1 shows an upper turning tone, and measure 2 shows a lower turning tone. The third type of unstressed nonharmonic tones is the *anticipation* (a), which may be reached by step or leap and is introduced just before it becomes a tone of the next chord:

Such standard ornaments as the *trill*, the *mordent*, and the *turn* are nothing but turning tones: the first a repeated upper turning tone, the second a lower turning tone, and the last an upper turning tone followed by a lower turning tone:

Other combinations of the three types of nonharmonic tones are also frequent.   For example:

In the last example the second turning tone is a turning tone of the first turning tone.

In the following exercises observe

Procedure 3 :

When soprano is given:
a. Determine the harmonies implied by it.
b. Write all the bass tones.
c. Add the middle parts.
d. Determine the type of nonharmonic tones used and add a symbol (p, t, a) above each.

When bass is given:
a. Write the soprano, using only chord tones.
b. Add the middle parts.
c. Add nonharmonic tones in the soprano (or elsewhere) and write a symbol (p, t, a) above each.

EXERCISES

1. Add the remaining two voices in the following exercises.   (In exercise t the position of the middle parts within the first chord may be changed.)

2. To the given soprano add the three lower parts, using only IV–V, V–IV, and IV–V–I progressions.   Write figures I, i, IV, iv, and V; accidentals for the leading tones in Minor; and symbols, p, t, a.   (In exercise g use contrary motion in the bass for the last two beats; such *contrary octaves* are best employed only at endings.)

3. To the given basses add the three upper parts and embellish one of them, naming the type of nonharmonic tones employed as before.

b : CADENCES AND HARMONIZATION OF MELODIES

(1) : Authentic and Plagal Cadences

As we saw in Chapter 6, section a(1), a single triad may belong to several keys. A tonality becomes clearly established only when all its tones have been heard. This may be done scale-wise, melodically, or with the help of several chords, harmonically. In order to sound seven tones, at least three triads are needed. When three such triads follow each other but do not end on the tonic triad, a strong tension is created, a longing to fall back to the tonic to rest there. When this tendency is carried out, the resulting chord sequence is called a *cadence*, that is, a "fall" (from Latin: cádere = to fall).

The tonic, subdominant, and dominant triads, followed again by the tonic, form the most usual cadence, the one with the strongest root progressions: two by fourths and one by an ascending second. These three chords are called the *primary harmonies*, or functions:

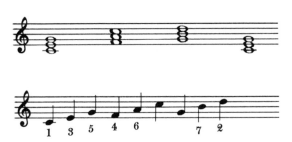

These three triads include all the steps of the scale, and the two most important ones — tonic and dominant — appear in two chords each, while the other scale steps appear only once:

When a cadence ends with V–I, it is known as an *authentic* cadence, and when it ends with IV–I, as a *plagal* cadence. The former is more vigorous because it contains the leading tone, which gives forceful direction to the chord sequence. Once a key has been established in a composition, a cadence may consist, incompletely, of only the two chords V and I. When the final tonic triad is in the position of the octave, a cadence is called *perfect*.

In order to give the effect of a cadence, the tonic triad which resolves the harmonic tension must come at the end of a phrase, usually on a strong beat; when this is not the case, no cadence is effected. When the dominant or subdominant triad is heard at the end of a passage, this produces a *half-cadence* — authentic when stopping on V, and plagal when stopping, more rarely, on IV. The cadence and the half-cadence are the musical counterparts to the period and the comma (or colon) in language.

EXERCISES

1. Write complete authentic cadences, I–IV–V–I, in strict connection, starting in all positions given under close and open harmony in Chapter 6, section a(2), and using figures I, i, IV, iv, and V in: F, f, F♯, f♯, G, g, A♭, g♯.

2. Using the same positions at the start, write complete plagal cadences, I–V–IV–I, in: A, a, B♭, b♭, a♯, B, b, c.

3. Add the three upper parts, the figures, and the names of the keys to the following basses. Use embellishments in the soprano and only strict connections.

(2) : *Harmonization of Melodies*

When harmonizing melodies it is good to heed the following suggestions:

Suggestion 3 :

Do not normally use more harmonies per measure than there are beats (for this purpose $^6_8$ has two beats), except occasionally in the next to last measure where tension is building up toward the cadence.

Suggestion 4 :

The fewer harmonies used, the more clearly the melody will be heard, but using too few harmonies may result in boredom.

Suggestion 5 :

Generally, do not have the same harmony on a weak beat and on the succeeding strong beat.

Suggestion 6 :

When a melody tone is held or repeated, this pause in melodic motion may well be used for a change in harmony (cf., suggestion 2, in Chapter 6b(2)).

In the following exercises all nonharmonic tones are indicated by "+." In deciding what triad to use with each of the chord tones, consult the examples given in section b(1) of this chapter. Those examples show that five of the seven steps of a scale belong to only one of the primary harmonies. The tonic and the dominant, however, may belong to either of two harmonies, and here the correct harmony can usually be reasoned out as well as heard — the student should do both.

EXERCISES

1. Employ procedure 3 (see section a of this chapter) and add figures to the bass. In exercise b use contrary octaves at the end (see section a, exercise 2g).

2. Do the same, but employ some nonharmonic tones in the three lower parts. In the first example use contrary octaves at the end (see section a, exercise 2g).

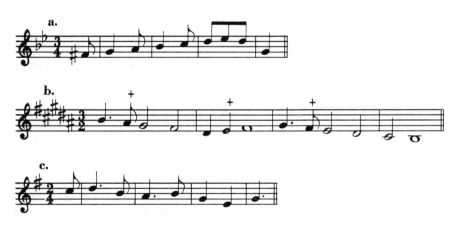

d.

e.

3. In the following melodies the nonharmonic tones are no longer indicated, except a few that .will be explained only subsequently and should here be supported by the same harmony as the preceding chord tone. Name all others by adding symbols p, t, or a. Instead of three additional melodic parts employ free pianistic accompaniments, such as the following (see Chapter 6, section b(1), exercise 4):

In these exercises upbeats need not be harmonized at all; appropriate rests will suffice.

a. *Dixie Land* (HC 6)

b. *Auld Lang Syne* (HC 12)

c. *O No, John* (HC 32, transposed)

d. *Silent Night* (HC 120, transposed)

e. *The Hundred Pipers* (HC 45)

f. *The Parable of the Sinful Rich Man* (HC 63)

c : MELODY WRITING

(1) : General Characteristics of Melody

When a number of consecutive musical tones is heard as a unit, one speaks of *melody*. In order to constitute a melody, tones have to be intelligibly tied together. The intelligibility of a melody is the result of (1) characteristic features as explained in the following section and (2) correspondences among the tones, such as repetitions, similarities, and particular groupings. The two musical elements which help most in producing such characteristic features or correspondences are melos and rhythm.

Melos is the pitch movement, or the motion of the tones, considered apart from rhythm. While the most pleasing vocal melodies are preponderantly stepwise in motion, the repeated use of characteristic intervals or leaps, particularly in instrumental melodies, will often help to make a melody effective.

The over-all melic aspect of a group of tones is called its *contour*. The more clearly the contour expresses direction, the more satisfactory will the melody be. A melody should have a definite rise and fall and should not hover around one pitch.

Suggestion 6 :

Except when skipping through the tones of a triad, rarely use in short melodies more than two skips, or one skip and two steps, or four steps in the same direction.

Suggestion 7 :

Only once in the course of a melody should a highest tone, or climax, be reached. A single lowest tone, or anticlimax, is also desirable.

Suggestion 8 :

To be pleasing and singable, a melody should hardly ever have a range (the interval between the highest and lowest tones) of less than a sixth or more than an octave and a sixth.

Rhythm is the lifeblood of melody. In fact, it is often easier to recognize a melody by its rhythm alone than by its melos. Characteristic rhythmic features will render a melody interesting, and their recurrence is very pleasing, if not overdone. Usually the note values become smaller before the final measure or measures of a melodic unit, indicating an increase of tension (concurrently with the start of the cadence) which relaxes on longer notes at the end of the unit. For example:

faster motion   longer note

(2) : Formulation of Melodies

A characteristic interval, group of intervals, or rhythmic formula, when it is repeated and remains recognizable under slight modifications, forms the smallest musical unit, which is called a *motif*.

Suggestion 9 :
In general, no striking feature in a melody should occur only once, for it would stand out awkwardly or unreasonably.

The next larger musical unit is the *phrase*. While a motif has an average length of one measure or less, a phrase may consist of two to six measures (sometimes more) and is comparable to a clause in speech. The length of a phrase is determined by the occurrence of a cadence. When a phrase is fairly long and practically constitutes a tune, the starting motif should be repeated somewhere. When the phrase is rather short, it will usually be followed by one or more phrases, each with its own cadence, before a stronger cadence intervenes; in such a case the repetition of motifs may be farther spaced to set up correspondences among the phrases.

The larger unit formed by a series of phrases is called a *period;* it corresponds to the sentence in speech. The starting phrase of a period is called the *antecedent* phrase, and the last one is the *consequent* phrase.

Sometimes there are several antecedent phrases and as many as two consequent phrases.   The observance of suggestions 7 and 8 is important with regard to both phrases and periods.

In the following exercises the consequent phrase may start in two ways, namely, by taking up the rhythm (and often also the melos) of either the beginning or the end of the antecedent (in either an identical or a slightly modified form).   Use both approaches with each exercise.

EXERCISES

1. Complete the following melodies by writing two consequent phrases for each, using the two approaches mentioned in the preceding paragraph.

Procedure 4 :

a. Clap the rhythm of the melody and find a pleasing rhythm for the consequent phrase.

b. Add notes to the rhythmic scheme thus established with some melodic correspondences and consideration for the over-all contour.

c. Having worked out each exercise in two versions, compare the result with the composer's solution, given after the exercises.

a. Mendelssohn — *Song Without Words, no. 23, op. 53, no. 5*

b. Mendelssohn — *Song Without Words, no. 13, op. 38, no. 1*

c. Mendelssohn — *Song Without Words, no. 36, op. 67, no. 6*

d. Mendelssohn — *Song Without Words, no. 14, op. 38, no. 2*

e. Beethoven — *Sonata in A, no. 2, op. 2, no. 2, second movement*

f. Mozart — *Piano Concerto in F, K. 459, third movement*

g. Handel — *Suite no. 7, Sarabande*

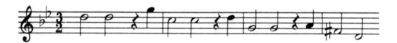

h. Schubert — *Impromptu in E♭, op. 90, no. 2, trio*

i. Schubert — *Impromptu in G, op. 90, no. 3*

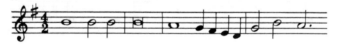

j. Schubert — *Impromptu in A♭, op. 142, no. 2*

k. Schubert — *Impromptu in Bb, op. 142, no. 3*

The following are the continuations of the above melodies:

2. Compose two-phrase periods of varying lengths (in numbers of measures), starting with the following motifs. Use each motif for two or more melodies. Among the melodies given in exercise 1, some close on the dominant and others on the third of the tonic triad, since they are parts of larger works. On the other hand, the following exercises should normally end on the tonic.

8

PRIMARY SIX-CHORDS†

a : ROOT PROGRESSIONS BY FOURTHS

The root of a chord need not be its bass tone. Whenever another chord tone is in the bass, we speak of an *inversion* of the chord. For example, in the chord

the notes cannot be arranged in thirds above the bass; in order to do so, the c^2 has to be inverted below the e^1, whereupon the chord is seen to be a C I triad with its third in the bass.

A triad has three tones. It can therefore appear in root-position and in two inversions. The first inversion, to which this chapter is devoted, has the third in the bass, and the second inversion has the fifth in the bass. Like the root-positioned triad, the triad in the first inversion may be in the position of the third (with the third of the triad in the soprano), fifth, or octave, and in open, close, or mixed harmony:

† Also spelled "sixth-chords."

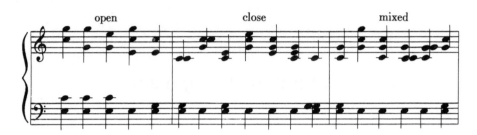

In inversions the tones are no longer arranged in thirds above the bass tone. Reduced to small intervals, the first inversion of a triad has a third and a sixth above the bass tone. During the seventeenth and eighteenth centuries, composers of vocal and instrumental solos used to write out only the solo melody and the bass of the accompaniment, leaving it to the accompanist to improvise the accompaniment from the bass line. To help him in this task, a type of musical shorthand was adopted to indicate the intentions of the composer. This shorthand is known as *figured bass*, which is a bass written out in notes with figures beneath it. The figures under a bass tone specify the intervals that should be played simultaneously with it and above it. In figured bass only those intervals are usually indicated that deviate from the third and the fifth of root-positioned triads. Thus a "6" beneath the bass indicates a sixth above that tone. This sixth excludes the fifth, but it still implies the usual third, which may be also indicated by a figure: $\frac{6}{3}$. The "6," or "$\frac{6}{3}$," is the appropriate indication for the first inversion of any triad, which is therefore called the *six-chord* (or six-three chord).

To create a smoother bass, a six-chord may be used for any triad, except at the very end of a piece and only rarely at the beginning. In primary six-chords (I_6, IV_6, and V_6) the doubling of the third (the bass tone) is best avoided because it obscures the feeling for the root of the chord, but both root and fifth are equally well doubled. In order to observe rule 1 (Chapter 6, section b), observe procedure 1 (*ibid.*) in strict connections of root progressions by fourths involving six-chords, modifying it only by reading: "a. Write the bass progression."

EXERCISES

1. Determine position (of 3rd, 5th, or 8ve) and type of harmony (open, close, or mixed) of all root-positioned triads and six-chords in "O No, John" (HC 32).

2. Connect strictly the following progressions and add the Roman numerals.
Then play them on the piano.

3. Connect strictly the following progressions and add the Roman numerals. Then play them on the piano.

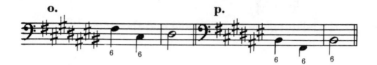

4. a. Expand the cadence I–IV–I–V–I in the following keys by interpolating after each of the first four triads its six-chord, making the cadence I–I₆–IV–IV₆–I–I₆–V–V₆–I: A, c, Eb, f♯, Bb, c♯, E, g. Use strict connections only, but employ nonharmonic tones in the melody. Start in different positions and alternately in open and close harmony.

b. Do the same with the cadence I–V–I–IV–I in: B, d, F, g♯, C, eb, Gb, a.

5. a. Play the root of a major triad in the left hand together with all three tones in the right hand. Play this in all positions, as follows; then transpose it all by ascending half-tones through an octave:

b. Do the same with a minor triad.

6. Do the right-hand portion of the preceding exercise with the left hand, using the fingering: 5–3–1, 5–3–1, 5–2–1.

7. Harmonize the following melodies with the help of such progressions as those given in exercise 4, but use pianistic accompaniments like those shown in Chapter 7, section b(2), exercise 3.

a. *Drink to Me Only with Thine Eyes* (HC 33)

b. *The Keeper* (HC 28)

c. Schubert — *Sonata in A, no. 9, op. posth., fourth movement*

d. Schubert — *Aufenthalt, op. posth.*

e. Schubert — *Frühlingsglaube, op. 20, no. 2*

f. Schubert — *Der Musensohn, op. 92, no. 1*

g. Schumann — *Aus meinen Tränen spriessen, op. 48, no. 2*

h. Schumann — *Die feindlichen Brüder, op. 49, no. 2*

i. Schumann — *Album Leaf I, op. 99*

8. Use such progressions as those given in exercise 4 to harmonize original melodies of two or three phrases on the following motifs:

b : ROOT PROGRESSIONS BY SECONDS

In order to observe rule 1 in stepwise root progressions involving six-chords, procedure 2 (Chapter 6, section c) must be amended to:

Procedure 2a :

    a. Write the bass progression.

    b. Complete the first chord.

    c. Write the progression of the roots or that of the fifths in another part.

    d. Lead one of the remaining voices (and, if possible, both of them) in contrary motion to the part written in c.

EXERCISES

1. Connect strictly the following progressions and add the Roman numerals. Then play them on the piano.

The progression IV₆–V in Minor, as used in exercises f, l, and p, is called the
Phrygian cadence.

2. Two things often make the otherwise difficult connections of IV₆ and V₆
possible: the bass tone (the third) of the IV₆ may be doubled (as in the progressions marked "1)" in the following exercises), and in Minor the melodic,
or natural, scale may be involved (as in the progressions marked "2)" in the

following exercises).   Connect the following progressions strictly and add the Roman and Arabic numerals.   Then play them on the piano.

3. a. Expand the cadence I–IV–V–I in the following keys by interpolating after each of the first three triads its six-chord to make it I–I₆–IV–IV₆–V–V₆–I: D♭, e, G, b♭, D, f, A♭, b.   Use strict connections only, but employ nonharmonic tones in the soprano.

   b. Do the same with I–V–IV–I in: d♯, F♯, a♭, C♭, a♯, C♯.

4. Harmonize the following melodies with the help of such progressions as those given in exercise 3, but employ pianistic accompaniments like those shown in Chapter 7, section b(2), exercise 3.   Play and check each exercise on the piano.

a. Schubert — *Der Lindenbaum, op. 89, no. 5*

b. Schubert — *Die Taubenpost, op. posth.*

c. Schubert — *Am Meer, op. posth.*

d. Schumann — *Aus alten Märchen winkt es, op. 48, no. 15*

e. Schumann — *Es treibt mich hin, op. 24, no. 2*

f. Schumann — *Tragödie II, op. 64, no. 3*

g. Mendelssohn — *Song Without Words, no. 28, op. 62, no. 4*

5. a. Use such progressions as those given in exercise 3 to support original melodies on the following motifs:

b. Use such progressions to harmonize similar melodies with accompaniments in free pianistic style (see Chapter 7, section b(2), exercise 3) using the following motifs:

9

THE DOMINANT SEVEN-CHORD†

a : THE V₇

(1) : Structure of the V₇

The construction of triads from two thirds suggests the possibility of adding another third to a triad. Between the root of such a four-tone chord and the added tone there is an interval of a seventh, a fact indicated by a "7" in figured bass. Such chords are therefore called *seven-chords*. They may be constructed on any step of a scale, but we shall limit ourselves at first to the one on the fifth step, the *dominant seven-chord* (V₇), all others being called *secondary seven-chords*.

Since the third of the dominant triad in Minor is taken over from the tonic Major, tonic Majors and Minors share not only identical V triads but also identical V₇ chords. For example,

C V₇: and c V₇:

There are, therefore, only twelve different V₇ chords (although there are more in notation), one constructed on each tone of the octave.

The *two essential characteristics of the V₇* are a major third and a minor seventh. The third is the leading tone of the key and has to

† Also spelled "seventh-chord."

move, whenever possible, to the tonic in the next harmony (see rule 2, Chapter 6, section b(1)). A tension in the chord is set up by the seventh, which is a comparative dissonance — a foreign element in the chord, a nonharmonic tone — which seeks to relax or resolve into a neighboring chord tone. Historically speaking, the seventh became part of the chord only long after it had been employed as a passing tone in this manner:

The seventh is therefore resolved best when it drops stepwise or is held over into the next chord. Occasionally the seventh moves stepwise up, but it never leaps, for dissonance and leaps both create stress, and adding one to the other results in an unpleasant overemphasis.

EXERCISES

1. Play the V₇ chord of C Major and Minor, with the fingering as shown below; then transpose it by ascending half-tones through an octave, first with one hand, then with the other:

2. Play the same V₇ chord in arpeggio with alternating hands as in the following example; then transpose it by ascending half-tones through an octave:

(2) : Stressed Dissonances and Hidden Octaves

In general, the following types of stresses are important in our study:

1. Melodic
   a. Skips
   b. Ascent

2. Harmonic
   a. Entrance of a new harmony
   b. Tension of either a leading tone or a dissonance

3. Contrapuntal
   a. Heard in the soprano and, secondarily, the bass
   b. Sounding of an octave or a fifth

In order to keep the flow of the four parts fairly evenly balanced, it is best to avoid combining too many stresses in one progression. From this observation spring the following rules:

Rule 4 :

A harmonically stressed dissonant tone, that is, one heard as a new harmony enters, should not be left by leap.

Rule 5 :

The dissonant intervals of a seventh and a ninth should be neither reached in similar motion from an octave nor left in similar motion going to an octave when involving a leap in the soprano.

Thus the following progressions are good:

and the following progressions are not good:

The last two progressions are often called *hidden octaves*, because they are heard as follows:

The F in these progressions is heard as a nonharmonic tone belonging to G.

In general, a hidden octave or, similarly, a hidden fifth is defined as an octave or a fifth reached in similar (but not parallel) motion. Unlike texts which forbid all hidden octaves and fifths, we will exclude only certain hidden octaves: those, like the ones in the preceding examples, that carry additional stresses, such as involving a leap up in the soprano. The following hidden octaves, for instance, are permitted:

All hidden fifths are also permitted:

(3) : The Complete V₇ and Its Resolution

Since the seven-chord has four tones, none can be doubled in four-part harmony. As for their arrangement, the chord may be in the position of the third, the fifth, or the seventh, and in open, close, or mixed harmony.

The V_7 may be used wherever a V triad can stand, but it is preferably spared for the final cadence, in which it sets up a higher tension

before the final tonic triad.   In moving from the V₇ to other chords,
follow

Procedure 6 :

 a. Write the bass progression.
 b. Lead the seventh stepwise down, hold it over, or, when the next chord is
I₆, lead it stepwise up to avoid bad hidden octaves.
 c. Take the leading tone to the tonic, especially when in the soprano.
 d. Take the remaining tone (the fifth) to the nearest tone of the next chord or
to one needed in it.

The first of these progressions shows that the *complete V₇* will, in strict
connection, resolve to an *incomplete I* with tripled root.   This progression must be practiced carefully before freer connections are used.

(4) : *The Incomplete V₇ and Its Resolution*

The only tone that may be omitted from a triad is the fifth (see Chapter
6, section b(2)); this is also the only nonessential tone in the V₇.   When
it is omitted in the *incomplete V₇,* one tone must be doubled.   Since
the third (the leading tone) and the seventh must both move in certain
prescribed ways so that parallel octaves would result from doubling
either, the only tone that may be doubled is the root.   Accordingly,
the incomplete V₇ may appear in octave position as well as in the
positions of the third and the seventh.   It resolves strictly to a complete I and is therefore often preferable to the complete V₇ in the
cadence.   Similarly, the incomplete V₇ is preferable in the connection
V₇–IV because it permits smoother voice leading.

Examples:

EXERCISES

1. Let each of the following tones serve as the root of a V_7 chord, alternating between complete and incomplete V_7 chords in all possible positions and distributions of middle parts, and determine to which keys each chord belongs: C, F, A♭, D♭, E, A, C♯, F♯, A♯, D♯, G♭, D, G, B♭, E♭, G♯, B, E♯.

The signs "(1)," "(2)," "(3)," and "(4)," which appear in exercises 2–6, apply respectively to the following instructions: (1) The perfect fifth may move to a diminished fifth or vice versa. (2) The seventh cannot be resolved downward because of bad hidden octaves (see rule 5 above) and must move stepwise up. (3) The incomplete V_7 is to be used. (4) The third should be doubled (see Chapter 8, section b, exercise 2).

The indices "$_3$," "$_5$," or "$_8$" at the beginnings of the exercises indicate a root-positioned triad in the position of the third, fifth, or octave respectively.

2. Write the following strict progressions:

   a. D I_8–V_7–I   **d.** e i_6–V_7–i

   b. f i_3–V_7–i   **e.** G I_3–V_7–I_6

   c. A I_5–$V_7^{(1)}$–I   **f.** b i_6–$V_7^{(2)}$–i

3. Write the following strict progressions and add the names of the keys and the Roman numerals:

4. Write the following strict progressions:

     a. B♭ $I_5–V_7{}^{(3)}–IV$ **d.** c $i_6–V_7–iv_6$

     b. c♯ $i_8–V_7{}^{(3)}–iv$ **e.** E $I_6–V_7–IV_6$

     c. F $I_3–V_7{}^{(3)}–IV$ **f.** g $i_3–V_7–iv_6$

5. Write the following cadences with strict treatment of the V_7 and add the names of the keys and the Roman numerals:

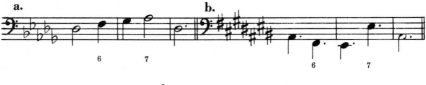

6. Write the following cadences with strict treatment of the V_7:

     a. C $I–V_6–IV_6{}^{(4)}–V_7–I$

     b. G♭ $I–I_6–IV–V_7–IV_6{}^{(4)}–V_6–I$

     c. d $i–i_6–iv–V_7–iv_6{}^{(4)}–V_6–i$

     d. A♭ $I–IV_6{}^{(4)}–V_6–V_7–I$

     e. e♭ $i–V–iv–i_6–iv_6–V_7–i$

7. Harmonize the following melodies with the aid of similar progressions and use some free pianistic accompaniments:

a. Mozart — *Sonata in A, K. 331, first movement*

b. Mozart — *Don Giovanni, Finale of Act II*

c. Mozart — *The Marriage of Figaro, Act I, no. 3, Se vuol ballare*

d. Mozart — *The Marriage of Figaro, Act II, no. 12, Venite, inginocchiatevi*

e. Mozart — *The Marriage of Figaro, Act IV, no. 27, Deh vieni, non tardar*

f. *The Ash-Grove* (HC 37)

g. *The Mansion We Builded* (HC 66)

8. Write original melodies using the following motifs, and harmonize them using progressions similar to those in the preceding exercises.

(5) : *Complete Resolutions of the Complete V₇*

Although the complete V₇ normally resolves to an incomplete I, under certain circumstances it can also resolve to a complete I, especially at endings. These circumstances are: (1) The leading tone must be in a middle part, so that it need not resolve to the tonic. (2) If possible, the part above the one sounding the leading tone should move to the tonic immediately above that leading tone. Accordingly, of the following examples the first is possible, but the second is better:

These resolutions should be sparingly used and only at endings.

EXERCISES

1. Write and play on the piano V₇–I progressions of both the types shown above, with the leading tone in the alto, in B, c♯, E♭, f, G, a.

2. Do the same, but with the leading tone in the tenor, in B♭, c, D, e, F♯, g♯.

b : INVERSIONS OF THE V₇

Like the triad, the seven-chord can occur with any of its tones in the bass. As with the triad, one speaks of root position when the root is in the bass and of inversions when any other tone is found there. Since the seven-chord has four tones, there are three inversions of it — the first with the third in the bass, the second with the fifth in the bass, and the third with the seventh in the bass. Their names are derived from the numerical symbols of figured bass, as follows:

The first inversion is called the *six-five-chord*, the third being implied by the fifth; the second inversion is the *four-three-chord*, with the sixth implied by the fourth; and the third inversion is known as the *two-chord*, as the second implies both fourth and sixth.   Only the numbers that figure in these names are commonly written as numerical symbols, and they are easily remembered: 7, 6–5, 4–3, and 2.   In Minor, where the sixth of the four-three-chord and the fourth of the two-chord are raised, the sixth and fourth respectively are added to these numerical symbols, together with the appropriate symbol to indicate the accidental: $^{6\sharp}_{4}_{3}$ or $^{4\natural}_{2}$.   Often the raised tone is indicated by an oblique line through the number: $^{\slashed{4}}_{3}, \slashed{2}$.

All the rules and procedures given in section a apply to the inversions of the V_7.   Therefore, since the leading tone naturally rises to the tonic (see procedure 6, step c, in section a(3)), the six-five-chord usually resolves to I rather than to I_6 or IV_6 (and to I_6 and IV_6 only in Major), and never to IV.   When the six-five-chord moves to I_6, the seventh will rise stepwise (see procedure 6, step b):

Good:

Possible:

Bad:

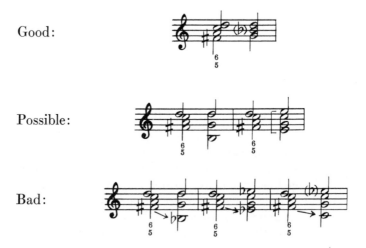

Observe the faulty bass progressions in the last group of examples.

Similarly, since the seventh normally descends stepwise (see procedure 6, step b), the two-chord usually resolves to I_6, occasionally to IV, but never to I or IV_6:

Good:

Possible:

Bad:

Whenever the fourth step of a scale occurs in a given bass, it can mean V_2 only when it moves stepwise down, continues into the next harmony, or jumps to another tone of the V_7 chord, for any inversion of a chord may be followed or preceded by any other inversion or the root position of the same chord.

Whereas the V_5^6 and V_2 have definitely preferred resolutions, the V_3^4, with the fifth in the bass, is free to move at will. When it proceeds to I_6, the seventh will usually ascend stepwise:

Poor:

EXERCISES

1. Play the root of the V_7 chord of C Major and Minor in the left hand together with all four tones in the right hand. Play this in all positions, as follows; then transpose it all by ascending half-tones through an octave:

2. Do the right-hand portion of the preceding exercise with the left hand, using the fingering: 5–3–2–1, 5–4–2–1, 5–3–2–1, 5–4–2–1.

3. Write the following chords and lead each to all good and possible resolutions among I, I_6, IV, and IV_6: A V_5^6; f# V_3^4; Eb V_2; c# V_5^6; Bb V_3^4; g V_2.

4. Write the following progressions and use nonharmonic tones to make the soprano more interesting:

    a. c i_6–IV–V_5^6–i   **f.** e iv_6–i–V_3^4–i_6

    b. B I–IV_6†–V_5^6–I   **g.** D I–V_5^6–IV_6–V_7–I

    c. a i_6–iv_6–V–$_2$V–i_6 **h.** bb i–IV_6†–V_5^6–i

    d. Ab IV–I_6–V_3^4–I   **i.** F# I_6–V_3^4–IV_6–V

    e. F I–V_2–IV–I   **j.** c# i_6–V_3^4–iv–i

5. Harmonize the following melodies with the aid of similar progressions, using some free pianistic accompaniments:

    a. Schubert — *Des Müllers Blumen, op. 25, no. 9*

† In the progression IV_6–V_5^6, as in the connection IV_6–V_6, the doubling of the bass tone of IV_6 is usually necessary or favorable.   In Minor, the melodic scale is employed so that the bass tones move more smoothly by a whole-tone.

b. Schubert — *Mit dem grünen Lautenbande, op. 25, no. 13*

c. Schubert — *Die liebe Farbe, op. 25, no. 16*

d. Schubert — *In der Ferne, op. posth.*

e. Schubert — *Der Atlas, op. posth.*

f. Schubert — *Geheimes, op. 14, no. 2*

g. Schumann — *Freisinn, op. 25, no. 2*

h. Schumann — *Venetianisches Lied, op. 25, no. 17*

i. Schumann — *Im Rhein, im heiligen Strome, op. 48, no. 6*

j. J. S. Bach — *Aus meines Herzens Grunde* (BR 1)

k. J. S. Bach — *Ach Gott, vom Himmel sieh' darein* (BR 3)

1.   J. S. Bach — *O Gott, du frommer Gott* (BR 85)

10

APPROACHES TO MELODY (2)

a : FREE, UNSTRESSED NONHARMONIC TONES

In Chapter 7 three types of nonharmonic tones were introduced: passing tones (p), turning tones (t), and anticipations (a). So far we have treated the first two strictly; both have been permitted only when reached and left by step. But, like anticipations, passing tones and turning tones are often reached by leap or left in this manner. When this occurs, they will be called free passing tones and free turning tones, but it must be remembered that both must be *either* reached *or* left by step. The varieties of passing and turning tones and their abbreviations are:

1. Free passing tones *reached by leap* and left by step: p_{rl}
2. Free passing tones reached by step and *left by leap:* p_{ll}
3. Free turning tones *reached by leap* and left by step: t_{rl}
4. Free turning tones reached by step and *left by leap:* t_{ll}.

Otherwise, the descriptions of passing and turning tones remain as given in Chapter 7: A passing tone is reached and left in the same direction, either ascending or descending, and a turning tone is reached and left in opposite directions. Some examples of free passing and turning tones follow:

The descending p₁₁ should be used with care; it is often not quite satis-factory. The upper t_{11}, on the other hand, is so characteristic and frequent that it has a name of its own: "escape tone" or "*échappée*." The lower t_{11} may be called an inverted *échappée*.

All nonharmonic tones are understood only in relation to a chord tone which is of the same pitch or one step higher or lower. In other words, unattached, completely "free" nonharmonic tones do not exist in traditional music. Some unstressed nonharmonic tones are, how-ever, reached *and* left by skip, for they are so well understood that instead of their usual resolution another chord tone may be substituted. We shall call this a *resolution by substitution*. Two examples will clarify this procedure:

Here a free passing tone, which should resolve to E, leaps away, for the sake of a fresh effect, to C.

An anticipation here assumes the appearance of a free passing tone.

There are many ornaments that combine several of these free passing and turning tones:

The last of these figures, particularly when composed of longer note values, is also known as *nota cambiata*, and defined as a four-note figure, the first and last notes of which are chord tones, descending usually by a third, and connected by a p_{ll} and a t_{rl}.† Therefore, the next-to-the-last figure may be called an inverted *cambiata*.

EXERCISES

1. Analyze the following excerpts for nonharmonic notes.   Add symbols for the harmonies and for the nonharmonic notes.

a. Chopin — *Etude in F Minor, op. 25, no. 2*

b. Chopin — *Prelude in G Major, no. 3*

† The student must be warned that this figure, as well as other nonharmonic tones, has been variously defined and named by different authors.

c. Chopin — *Waltz in B Minor, no. 10*

d. Haydn — *Sonata in C Major (1780), finale*

2. Write the middle parts into the following phrases and ascribe to each non-harmonic note the correct symbol.   Then play each phrase on the piano.

b : STRESSED NONHARMONIC TONES

As there are three types of unstressed nonharmonic tones, there are also three stressed types. By stress we refer primarily to the entrance of a new harmony but also to the comparatively strong beat. A stressed nonharmonic tone is one heard either as a new harmony enters or on a comparatively strong beat. The three stressed types of nonharmonic tones are: the *appoggiatura* (A), the *suspension* (S), and the *pedal point* (P).

(1) : The Appoggiatura

The appoggiatura† is defined as a stressed nonharmonic tone reached by step or leap and left by step. In its various forms it may be called a stressed (strict or free) passing or turning tone left by step. To each appoggiatura, moreover, may be ascribed a numerical name derived from the figured bass. Thus:

† From the Italian *appoggiare* = to lean (toward the resolution).

would be called a 4–3 appoggiatura, although functionally it represents a 6–5 movement of the stressed t_{r1} type.   Similarly,

is a 9–10 appoggiatura of the stressed passing tone variety; the numbers 2–3 are usually reserved to refer to a melodic progression in the tenor.

The two tones involved in the appoggiatura are known as the appoggiatura and the resolution.   The actual pitch of the resolution should never be heard simultaneously with the appoggiatura, and it is normally best to avoid placing the resolution in any lower octave while the appoggiatura is sounded, particularly when the latter resolves by a half-tone step.   When appoggiatura and resolution are heard at the same time, the resolution is best placed in the bass or in a voice higher than the one in which the dissonance occurs.

(2) : The Suspension

The suspension is closely related to the appoggiatura, and the preceding paragraph applies to suspensions and their resolutions as well as to appoggiaturas.   A suspension is a stressed nonharmonic tone reached by *prolongation* and left by step.   Prolongation means that the nonharmonic tone is actually the continuation of a chord tone heard in the preceding harmony, which in this instance is known as the *preparation*.   A slight modification of the preceding musical example turns it into a suspension, with its three constituents — the preparation, the suspension, and the resolution:

The suspension may also be described as a prepared appoggiatura, and, conversely, the appoggiatura may be described as an unprepared suspension.

According to a traditional rule, the preparation must be at least as long as the suspension; if it is shorter it is referred to as an anticipation, and the suspension becomes an appoggiatura. Usually the preparation is tied to the suspension, but it need not be; if it is not, some theorists insist on calling the figure an appoggiatura. A suspension that resolves upward is sometimes called a *retardation*. The numerical names of suspensions are, like those of appoggiaturas, derived from the figured bass (see the preceding musical example).

(3) : The Pedal Point

The pedal point is a stressed nonharmonic tone which is both reached and left by prolongation. The tone that becomes a dissonance is heard as a consonance in both the preceding and the following harmony:

Originally the name "pedal point" applied to the low bass tones of the organ pedals, but this type of dissonance may occur in any part and at any pitch.

It is easy to remember all the six types of nonharmonic tones as follows:

Unstressed: t-a-p   turning tone, anticipation, passing tone

Stressed: S-A-P   suspension, appoggiatura, pedal point

All are defined by (1) how they are reached and (2) how they are left, and some also by (3) the directions in which they are reached or left. It should be remembered that unstressed dissonances may be left by leap, but stressed dissonances, because they attract more attention, must be resolved stepwise or held over.

EXERCISES

1. Analyze the following excerpts for nonharmonic notes; add symbols for the harmonies and for all nonharmonic notes and ascribe the correct numerical symbols to each A and S:

a. Haydn — *Sonata in D Major (1767), first movement*

b. Haydn — *Sonata in E Major (1773), finale*

c. Haydn — *Sonata in E♭ Major (1780), first movement*

d. Haydn — *Sonata in E♭ Major (1790), finale*

e. Schubert — *Der Neugierige, op. 25, no. 6*

f. Schubert — *Der Müller und der Bach, op. 25, no. 19*

g. Schubert — *Frühlingsglaube, op. 20, no. 2*

2. Write the middle parts into the following phrases and ascribe to each non-harmonic note the correct symbol; then play each phrase on the piano:

a.

c : **COMBINATIONS OF NONHARMONIC TONES**

All types of nonharmonic tones may be horizontally (melodically) or vertically (harmonically or contrapuntally) combined.

Turning and passing tones or anticipations may be inserted between an appoggiatura or suspension and its resolution:

Passing and turning tones may be doubled, usually in parallel thirds or sixths:

Similarly, appoggiaturas and suspensions may be doubled, and such double suspensions may be combined with unstressed dissonances:

The variety of such combinations is very great. The student must check carefully by ear what he writes, because not every correct

usage is satisfactory in sound. The following rules should be kept
in mind:

Rule 6 :

*Every nonharmonic tone, being a dissonance, must be heard as related to a chord
tone on the same pitch or on one a single step away.*

Rule 7 :

*While unstressed dissonances need not resolve stepwise if they are so reached,
stressed dissonances must always be resolved stepwise or by prolongation.*

Rule 1 (Chapter 6, section b(1)) about avoiding parallel fifths and
octaves applies not only to the motion from two chord tones to two
chord tones but also to that from two nonharmonic tones to two nonharmonic tones and to the motion from two chord tones to two nonharmonic tones and vice versa. Otherwise nonharmonic tones normally neither disturb good progressions nor improve bad ones.

11

SIX-FOUR CHORDS

AND THE V_9 AND V_7^{13} CHORDS

a : SIX-FOUR CHORDS

In traditional music the second inversion of the triad, the six-four chord, was usually treated as though its fourth, or both its fourth and sixth, were nonharmonic tones. For the composers of the eighteenth and nineteenth centuries this chord did not possess the stable quality of the triad and the six-chord, but needed a resolution. When the six-four chord occurred on a strong beat, the fourth in particular and often also the sixth were treated like suspensions or appoggiaturas. When this chord occurred on a weak beat, the fourth was introduced as a passing or turning tone, and at times as an anticipation, often paralleled by the sixth. We shall therefore understand the six-four chords best as harmonies containing nonharmonic tones, and shall study them in the following order: (1) the appoggiatura (suspension) $_4^6$; (2) the passing $_4^6$; (3) the turning (pedal-point) $_4^6$; (4) the anticipation $_4^6$; and (5) the $_4^6$ as an incomplete triad as it occurs in pianistic accompaniments. These will be the only uses of this chord permitted in our study.

(1) : The Appoggiatura $_4^6$

The most frequent six-four chords are the so-called cadential ones: I_4^6 and IV_4^6. The I_4^6, with the dominant in the bass, acts as an appoggiatura before V or V_7. It should normally enter on a stronger beat than its resolution. Since it precedes V, it usually follows IV (also I or I_6). When I_4^6 follows IV, it should, since it represents V, be introduced in the same manner as V, according to the rule of contrary motion between IV and V. The fourth must always be resolved stepwise, like other appoggiaturas:

The IV_4^6, with the tonic in the bass, acts as an appoggiatura of I. Since the IV_4^6 precedes I, it normally follows a V chord of any type or form. Although the connection V–IV is somewhat weak, this progression is excellent. Here again the fourth must be resolved stepwise:

(2) : The Passing $_4^6$

The V_4^6 is not often used as an appoggiatura chord. It is more satisfactory in an unstressed position, between I and I_6 or vice versa, as a passing chord:

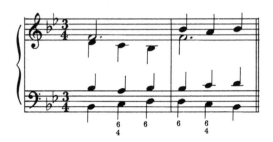

Similarly, the I_4^6 functions well in passing between IV and IV$_6$ or vice versa, and the IV_4^6 in passing between V_5^6 and V_3^4 and vice versa:

In all three cases the fourth is introduced by means of a passing motion in the bass, and even though the sixth may make a turning motion, it is best to call these chords passing six-fours.

(3) : The Turning $_4^6$

The I_4^6 and IV_4^6 frequently serve as turning chords:

The progression V–I_4^6–V$_7$ easily becomes a passing figure, involving the incomplete V$_7$ without the third:

Like unstressed nonharmonic tones in general, the fourth (and sixth) of the passing and turning six-four chords may be *either* reached *or* left by leap, but not both:

(4) : *The Anticipation* $^6_4$

The I$^6_4$ and IV$^6_4$ can also occur as anticipation chords:

(5) : *The* $^6_4$ *as Incomplete Triad*

Often simple accompaniments, such as those of marches and waltzes, will alternately sound the root or third of a chord on one beat and a full chord, usually in an inversion, on the next one or two beats.   The single tones and chords that form such a group must all be considered as parts of one chord, like the broken chords of free pianistic accompaniments shown in Chapter 7, section b(2), exercise 3, and, consequently, what sometimes appears to be a six-four chord is actually an incomplete chord. This is illustrated in the following example, which also shows that rather strict voice leading remains the best approach even in such "free" accompaniments:

EXERCISES

1. a. Write and play cadences of the form I–IV–I$_4^6$–V$_7$–I–IV$_4^6$–I in the following keys: B, b, A, a, G, g.

   b. Write and play cadences of the form I–IV$_6$–I$_4^6$–V$_5^6$–IV$_4^6$–I in the following keys: F, f, E♭, e♭, C♯, c♯.

   c. Write and play cadences of the form I–V$_4^6$–I$_6$–I$_4^6$–V$_3^4$–IV$_4^6$–I in the following keys: D, d, E, e, F♯, f♯.

   d. Write and play cadences of the form I–IV$_4^6$–I–IV–V–I$_4^6$–V$_7$–IV$_4^6$–I in the following keys: A♭, a♭, B♭, b♭, C, c.

2. Give a harmonic analysis, by ascribing the appropriate figured-bass symbols under each chord, of the first sections of Chopin's Waltzes No. 4 in F Major (measures 1–48) and No. 6 in D♭ Major (measures 1–20).

      b : THE V$_9$, V$_{11}$, AND V$^{13}_7$ AND THEIR INVERSIONS

Like the six-four chords, all chords discussed in this section may be described as including nonharmonic tones. These tones are so important and attract so much attention that they should be normally heard in the soprano. Placing them in any other part distracts so much from the melody that either an unsatisfactory sound results or one which is no longer identified with an accepted chord but only with a nonharmonic tone.

(1) : The V_9

The V_9 may be described as a V_7 with a 9–8 appoggiatura or suspension. The ninth is a major ninth in Major and a minor ninth in Minor. Consequently, although the V_7 chords of a tonic Major and Minor are identical, the V_9 chords are not. The ninth should always be (1) in the soprano (see the preceding paragraph) and (2) resolved stepwise downward or held over. The other tones resolve as in the V_7:

This chord contains five different tones. In the usual four-part settings the one tone which is omitted is the fifth, the only nonessential tone of the chord. This eliminates the problem of the doubled third or awkward parallel fifths when the V_9 resolves to a form of I:

Since neither the omitted fifth nor the ninth (which must be in the soprano) can be in the bass, the V_9 has only two possible inversions in four-part harmony: one with the third in the bass and one with the seventh in the bass, the $\begin{smallmatrix}7\\6\\5\end{smallmatrix}$ chord and the $\begin{smallmatrix}10\\4\\2\end{smallmatrix}$ chord respectively:

Because the pitch of the resolution should not be heard before the

actual resolution, the root of the V_9 must not be placed next to the
ninth, particularly not when the chord resolves to a form of I.   The
two inversions can therefore be used only in the arrangements shown
in the preceding example, except that the bass tone may be lowered
by an octave.   Similarly, the root position may occur in only two
forms, close and open:

The $V_{\frac{6}{5}}^{7}$, like the V_5^6, normally resolves to I or to IV_6 in Major; it
may also pass to the IV_4^6 or go to any other form of dominant.   The
$V_{\frac{4}{2}}^{10}$, like the V_2, resolves to I_6 or IV.   The V_9 may move to I, I_6, IV, or
IV_6 as we have seen, but when it goes to I_6 the seventh moves stepwise
up as in the progression V_7–I_6.

(2) : The V_{11} and V_{13}

The V_9 may be described as a V_7 with an added third.   Similarly, the
V_{11} may be said to be a V_9 with an added third.   This chord, which
occurred first in the romantic music of the nineteenth century, cannot
be employed in four-part settings, since it comprises six different tones,
all essential except the fifth.   We shall therefore not discuss it at
length, but merely state that the eleventh and ninth must be in the
soprano and alto (either may be on top), and both must be resolved
stepwise downward or held over.   Because the V_{11} is not used in the
traditional four-part setting, the symbols of its inversions have not
acquired general acceptance.

All that has been said about the V_{11} applies, with a few appropriate
changes, to the V_{13}.   This chord, which adds a third to the V_{11}, actually
contains all seven notes of the scale:

(3) : The V_7^{13}

In order to differentiate it from the V_{13}, the far more common four-tone chord which also contains the thirteenth is labeled V_7^{13}. It is a V_7 with a 6–5 appoggiatura, which, as the outstanding dissonance, is always in the soprano and is therefore called a thirteenth rather than a sixth. The thirteenth is a major thirteenth in Major and a minor thirteenth in Minor; thus, unlike the V_7 chords, the V_7^{13} chords of tonic Major and Minor differ:

Since the thirteenth is a 6–5 appoggiatura, it naturally resolves stepwise downward within the chord. However, when the chord proceeds to I or IV, the thirteenth may skip this resolution, which is so very common and expected, and move directly to the tonic by a skip of a third downward. Although this looks like an exception to rule 7 (Chapter 10, section c), which states that stressed nonharmonic tones must resolve stepwise, this leap across the normal stepwise resolution is accepted as correct, while the holding over of the thirteenth into the next chord is rarer:

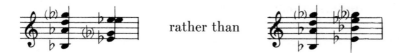

rather than

Because the fifth of the chord is represented by its appoggiatura, the thirteenth, it is not otherwise present in the V_7^{13}; and since the thirteenth must always be in the soprano, the V_7^{13} has only two inversions like the V_9: one with the third in the bass and one with the seventh in the bass, the $V^{11}_{\substack{6\\5}}$ and the $V^{7}_{\substack{4\\2}}$ respectively. Both of these and the root position occur in only two forms each:

The $V^{11}_{\substack{6\\5}}$, like the V^{6}_{5}, normally resolves to I or to IV_{6} in Major; it also may pass to IV^{6}_{4} or go to any other form of the dominant. The $V^{7}_{\substack{4\\2}}$, like the V_{2}, moves to I_{6} or IV. The V^{13}_{7} resolves to I, I_{6}, IV, or IV_{6}, but when resolving to I_{6}, the seventh moves stepwise up as in the progression V_{7}–I_{6}:

The V_{9} and V^{13}_{7} have several things in common:

1. The outstanding dissonance — ninth or thirteenth — must be in the soprano and never moves up.

2. Each has only two inversions: the first, derived from V^{6}_{5}: $V^{7}_{6\\5}$ and $V^{11}_{6\\5}$, and the third, derived from $V^{(4)}_{2}$: $V^{10}_{4\\2}$ and $V^{7}_{4\\2}$.

3. Each appears in only a few forms.

4. Each has a different form in Major and Minor.

EXERCISES

1. Write and play the following progressions:

a. c V_9–i

b. D V_5^6–I

c. e $V_2^{10}_4$–i$_6$

d. F♯ V_7^{13}–I

e. g♯ $V_5^{11}_6$–i

f. B♭ $V_2^7_4$–I$_6$

g. B V_9–I$_6$

h. c♯ $V_5^7_6$–i$_6$

i. E♭ $V_5^7_6$–IV$_6$

j. f $V_2^{10}_4$–iv

k. G V_7^{13}–I$_6$

l. a $V_5^{11}_6$–i$_6$

m. C $V_5^{11}_6$–IV$_6$

n. d $V_2^7_4$–iv

o. E V_9–IV

p. f♯ V_7^{13}–iv

q. A♭ V_9–IV$_6$

r. b♭ V_7^{13}–iv$_6$

2. a. Play C V_9 on the piano, then transpose the chord by ascending half-tones through an octave. Practice this chromatic progression until it is fluent, then do the same with C $V_5^7_6$ and $V_2^{10}_4$.

b. Do the same with C V_7^{13}, $V_5^{11}_6$, and $V_2^7_4$.

c. Do the same with C V_{11} and V_{13}.

d. Do the same with c V_9 and V_7^{13} and their inversions and with c V_{11} and V_{13}.

3. Using the given motifs in the soprano, work out the following figured basses. Use nonharmonic tones, particularly in the melody. Begin by writing in the soprano the necessary notes wherever a V_9 or V_7^{13} or one of their inversions occurs, and then lead the melody so as to incorporate these notes.

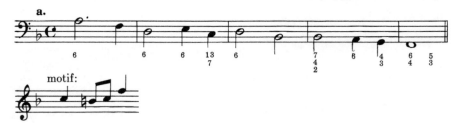

12

SECONDARY TRIADS

Up to this point only primary harmonies — I, IV, and V — have been studied. Despite this limitation, our cadences have become richer through the use of inversions, nonharmonic tones, and expansions of the V chord. New possibilities for enlarging and varying the cadence are introduced by the secondary triads. Their treatment, while not essentially different from that of the primary triads, involves some special features with respect to (1) chord structure and (2) desirable doublings.

(1) : Types of Triads

Let us first recall what types of triads are found on the various steps of Major and Minor (considering only harmonic Minor for the sake of simplicity):

Types of triads:	major	minor	diminished	augmented
In Major:	I, IV, V	ii, iii, vi	vii°	
In Minor:	V, VI	i, iv	ii°, vii°	III+

For the first time diminished and augmented triads will be involved in our settings. The diminished fifth of the diminished triad sounds rather weak when either tone of this fifth is in the bass.   Consequently, the root position and the six-four-chord of such triads are rarely used, the six-chord being preferable to either.

All three positions of the augmented triad sound alike, for all its intervals are major thirds.   For this reason there exist only four different augmented triads, except for enharmonic respellings.   Nevertheless, the six-chord of the augmented triad is more often employed than the other two forms, because the crucial augmented fifth, which involves the leading tone, is somewhat de-emphasized and loses some of its sharpness when heard above the third in the bass.

(2) : Doublings

With primary triads the best doublings are those of the root and fifth, but with secondary triads the doubling of the third is equally successful and is sometimes better than doubling the root or the fifth.   The reason for this is that the thirds of primary triads — the mediant in I, the submediant in IV, and the leading tone in V — are tonally of secondary importance, so that their doubling weakens the harmonic strength of these chords.   The thirds of secondary triads, on the other hand, are either tonally very important — the subdominant in II, the dominant in III, and the tonic in VI — or are the only tones usually available for doubling, as in VII and in II and III in Minor.   In the last three triads the tones that form the augmented or diminished fifth are not free to move, for such intervals are heard as expressing definite tendencies, like nonharmonic tones.   A diminished interval invites further contraction of that interval and an augmented one further expansion, so that the doubling of either tone would cause bad parallels or unsatisfactory progressions.   This leaves the thirds of the augmented and diminished triads as the best prospect for doubling:†

I   IV   V   ii   iii   vi   vii°   ii°   III⁺
i   iv   V   VI   vii°

† The rule found in many texts that the doubling of the third is better in minor triads than in major triads is incorrect.   It stems from the fact that in Major most secondary triads are minor triads and all primary ones are major triads.

b : TYPES OF PROGRESSIONS

So far we have used only root progressions by fourths and seconds. The introduction of secondary harmonies makes available the only remaining type of root progressions — root progressions by thirds. Some root progressions are stronger than others (see Chapter 6, section c(1)), and the order of root progressions, from strong to weak, is as follows: progressions (1) by fourths, (2) up by seconds, (3) down by thirds, (4) down by seconds, and (5) up by thirds.

Progressions down by seconds are actually heard as retrograde motion of the IV–V progression. They are particularly characteristic of Renaissance church music, and when they occur often in succession they evoke a feeling of church modality. Because root progressions by thirds always involve chords with two common tones and only one new one, they are not overly strong. In root progressions down by a third the new tone is the root of the second chord, which adds some freshness to this progression. In progressions up by a third, on the other hand, the root of the second chord is already heard in the first one, so that such progressions affect the listener as a harmonic standstill in which a seventh is simply added to a triad:

Such progressions are therefore poor in any context.

In all root progressions by fourths (*dominant* progressions) the procedures of voice leading studied in connection with the progressions I–IV and I–V should be observed. In progressions by seconds (*stepwise* progressions) the rules concerning IV–V and V–IV progressions apply. In progressions by thirds (*median* progressions) the holding of two tones is perfectly acceptable (sometimes even three tones may be held over), but it is equally good to use motion to avoid multiple prolongations.

c : PLACING OF SECONDARY HARMONIES

The cadences I–IV–(I–)V–I and I–V–(I–)IV–I are the basic formulas of Baroque and classic-romantic music. Secondary harmonies find

their places within these formulas in two ways: (1) as substitutes for
the three primary functions and (2) through a fifth-fall chain.

(1) : Substitutes for Primary Functions

We already know that any two triads of a key with roots a third apart
share two of their tones:

Any two such chords, called mediants, are so closely related that they
can represent each other. Thus the possible substitutes for the
primary harmonies may be listed as follows:

IV may be represented by II or VI
I may be represented by III or VI
V may be represented by III or VII

As this table indicates, **II** will always be heard as representing **IV**, and
VII as representing **V** (in fact, **VII** is but a **V₇** without root). The
other two secondary triads, **III** and **VI**, are ambiguous or neutral
harmonies, as either may represent two different primary functions.
However, **III⁺** in Minor is normally heard as representing **V**, because
it displays the leading tone conspicuously. When following **V**, **VI** is
usually heard as representing **I**; when following **I**, as representing **IV**.
A too frequent use of the neutral harmonies, **III** and **VI**, will weaken
the tonal feeling.

The most important ways in which these substitute harmonies
create variety in the cadence are the following.

Wherever a **IV** may be used in a cadence, a **II** or a **VI** may take
its place. Where any form of a **V** may be found, a **VII** or a **III** may
be placed, the latter best in six-chord position with the dominant in
the bass (in fact, the **III₆** is identical with the V^{13}_7 without its seventh).
When a cadence seems to reach its completion and the **V** is followed
by a **VI** (or less often a **III**) instead of the expected **I**, one speaks of a

deceptive cadence (which will be studied below in section d). Two or all three chords representing a primary function may be introduced in a group before the next primary function enters, and these chords are best handled in root progressions by descending fifths or thirds.

EXERCISES

1. Write the following cadences:

    a. A $I-vi-iii_6-I$

    b. f $i-VI-iv-vii^{\circ}_6-V^{13}_7-i$

    c. D♭ $I-vi-IV-ii-I^6_4-V^{6\,7}_5-I$

    d. a $i-vii^{\circ 7}_6-i^{\circ}_6-ii^{\circ}_6-VI_6-i-iv_6-ii^{\circ 6}_6-i^6_4-V^{7-}_{43}\dagger-iv^6_4-i$

2. Play these exercises on the piano and transpose each to three different keys, both major and minor.

3. Invent three similar cadences; write and play them.

(2) : The Fifth-Fall Chain

The progressions I–IV and V–I are examples of *fifth-falls*, which are root progressions by fourths up or fifths down. Such fifth-fall progressions are always effective. A chain of fifth-falls, one of them a progression by a diminished fifth, contains all the steps of a key: I–IV–VII–III–VI–II–V–I. Its bass is best arranged on the piano within an octave, as follows:

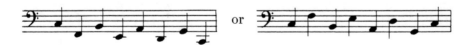

In this progression the triad built on any single scale step may be omitted, as well as any group of three, four, or five consecutive harmonies (but not two). It is therefore possible to derive all the simple

† This is a 4–3 suspension.

cadences, such as I–IV–(VII–III–VI–II–)V–I, I–(IV–VII–III–VI–)
II–V–I, I–IV–(VII–III–VI–II–V–)I, and I–IV–VII–(III–VI–II–V–)I,
from the fifth-fall chain by omitting the portions in parentheses.   On
the other hand, fifth-fall groups of any length may begin at any point
in a cadence and may be concluded by a cadence at any point.   In
addition, any harmony in the chain may be used in the form of an
inversion.

EXERCISES

Write the following exercises, using nonharmonic tones (particularly in the
soprano) to make each as musical as possible.   Use the piano for checking.

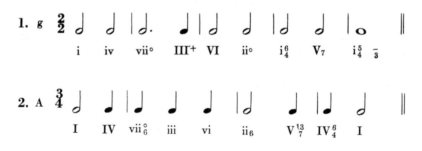

† In this progression it is best to avoid sounding the resolution and the suspension simultaneously
by leaping from the root of the V$^{11}_{6\ 5}$ to that of the I.

†† This is a 6–5 suspension.

d : THE DECEPTIVE CADENCE

The deceptive (or interrupted) cadence, particularly V–VI, is one of the most important devices for expanding a phrase. Where a phrase would be ended if I followed V, the deceptive cadence enables the phrase to expand and go on toward a second cadence.

Since V–VI is a stepwise root progression, it is best, as in IV–V, to lead the other parts in contrary motion to the progression of the roots. However, V includes the leading tone, which must rise, and this leads to a doubled third in VI:

This resolution also follows V_7 and V_7^{13}, but not V_9, which resolves to a VI with doubled root:

In Major the leading tone may, when in a middle part, descend to double the root of VI, but not in Minor, where this would mean a step of an augmented second:

Good:

Bad:

The resolution to VI with a doubled third is the most frequent and typical one, and it must be carefully practiced.

EXERCISES

1. Write and play the following cadences, using some nonharmonic tones in the soprano.

    a. C   I–ii$_6$–V$_7$–vi

    b. d   i$_6$–ii$_6^{\circ}$–V$_7^{13}$–VI

    c. E   I–IV$_6$–V$_5^6$–vi$_6$–ii$_6$–V$_3^4$–vi$_6$–I

    d. f$\sharp$ i–iv–V$_9$–VI

    e. A$\flat$ I–IV–I$_6$–V$\,_5^{\,6}\!\!{}^{11}$–vi–ii–iii$_6$–V$_7$–vi

2. Play the progressions C V–vi, c V–VI, C V$_7$–vi, and c V$_7$–VI in various positions. Transpose each by half-tones upward through an octave.

13

SECONDARY SEVEN-CHORDS

a : TYPES AND FUNCTIONS OF SEVEN-CHORDS

A seven-chord, like a triad, may be written on every step of a key. Considering only Major and harmonic Minor, Chapter 12, section a(1), showed that there were only four types of triads, each occurring on specific steps in either mode. Again considering only Major and harmonic Minor, there exist seven types of seven-chords, which occur on specific steps of these modes. These seven types of seven-chords can be easily remembered as derived from the four kinds of triads through the addition above each of either a minor or a major third:

Added third:
	M	m	M	m	M	m	(M)	m

Triad:
	M	M	m	m	d	d	(a)	a

	(1)	(2)	(3)	(4)	(5)	(6)	(6a)	(7)

Name of seven-chord:
major	major-	minor-	minor	half-	dimin-	( )	aug-
	minor	major		dimin-	ished		mented
	or V₇			ished			

Of the eight theoretically possible chords one (6a) cannot be realized, because the addition of a major third above an augmented triad results in merely doubling the root of that triad. Each of the other seven chords is characterized by, and therefore named after, its basic triad and the added third: (1) is the *major seven* (rather than calling it major-major because of its major triad and major third); (2) is the V_7, but it also occurs on steps other than V (such as on **IV** in melodic Minor) and is therefore better called the *major-minor seven* (major triad plus minor third); (3) is the *minor-major seven;* (4) is the *minor seven* (rather than calling it minor-minor); (5) is called (rather than diminished-major) the *half-diminished* seven in reference to (6), which is called the *diminished seven* (rather than diminished-minor) because it includes both a diminished fifth and a diminished seventh; and (7) is the *augmented seven* (rather than the augmented-minor) because there is only one seven-chord based on the augmented triad.

Since a particular seven-chord can occur only on a scale step on which its basic triad is found, the table given in Chapter 12, section a(1), will serve here again with only a few additions to account for the added major or minor third in each chord:

Triads:		major		minor		dimin.	augm.
Seven-chords:	major	major-minor	minor-major	minor	half-dimin.	dimin.	augm.
In Major:	I_7, IV_7	V_7		$ii_7, iii_7,$ vi_7	vii_7°		
In Minor: (harmonic)	VI_7	V_7	i_7	iv_7	$\overset{..}{ii}{}_7^\circ$	$vii_{7\flat}^\circ$	III_7^+

This table shows that, considering only Major and harmonic Minor, four of the seven-chords occur on only one step each: the V_7, i_7, $vii_{7\flat}^\circ$, and III_7^+. Consequently, these four chords easily identify a key, while the other three — the major, minor, and half-diminished seven-chords — are more neutral.

The inversions of any seven-chord have the same numerical names as those of the V_7: $\frac{6}{5}$, $\frac{4}{3}$, and $_2$.

EXERCISES

1. a. Name the type of each of the following chords, and identify each by key letter and Roman and Arabic numerals:

b. Play each of these chords on the piano and transpose it by half-tones upward through an octave.

2. a. Name the type of each of the following chords, and give all the possible key letters and Roman numerals for each:

b. Play each of these chords on the piano and transpose it by half-tones upward through an octave.

b : DOUBLINGS AND RESOLUTIONS

Only the third or the fifth can be omitted from any seven-chord. In seven-chords that include a perfect fifth, this is the best tone to omit; omitting the third, which can be done occasionally, may lead to doubt as to whether a major or a minor third was intended. In the half-diminished and augmented seven-chords only the third may be omitted, because the fifth is a characteristic interval. In the diminished seven-chord, which consists of three equal intervals (minor thirds), either the third or the fifth may be omitted.

Good:

Less good:

Correct:

Since seven-chords have four different tones, doublings are possible in four-part settings only when one tone is omitted. In such cases the best doubling is that of the root, but the third or the fifth may occasionally be doubled. The seventh and the diminished and augmented fifth should not be doubled because they have to move in certain ways and their doubling would lead to undesirable parallels. Therefore, any incomplete VII_7 is difficult to handle.

In general, the seventh of a seven-chord resolves stepwise down or is held into the next chord. It never leaps and rarely goes up, except when it is the leading tone, that is, in I_7 or i_7. The diminished fifth usually resolves downward, and the augmented fifth, being the leading tone, must rise. In the vii_7^{o} (the half-diminished) and particularly in the $vii_{7\flat}^{o}$ (the diminished) the root is the leading tone and normally rises.†

All these remarks do not constitute new rules but rather consequences of the usual treatment of the leading tone, the seventh, and diminished and augmented intervals. Similarly, all that has been said in Chapter 12 about secondary triads applies as well to the placing of secondary seven-chords in the cadence and to their progressions.

EXERCISES

1. In the following exercises use some nonharmonic tones in the soprano. Play all exercises on the piano and transpose each to at least two other keys.

a.

I I_7 vi_7 IV_7 ii_5^6 I_4^6 V_7 I

† In this book the diminished seven-chord, wherever it is specifically demanded, is symbolized by a flat as follows: $vii_{7\flat}^{o}$, $vii_{5\flat}^{o6}$, $vii_{3\flat}^{o4}$, except for its third inversion, vii_{2}^{o}.

b.

c.

d. c♯ $\frac{5}{8}$ i–vii$^{°4}_{3}$–III$^{+}_{7}$–i$_6$–iv$_2$–vii$^{°}_{7}$–VI$_6$–VI$_7$–iv$^{6}_{5}$–ii$^{°4}_{3}$–i$^{6}_{4}$–iv$_7$–V$^{5\ 7}_{4\ 3}$–VI–ii$^{°4}_{3}$–iv$_6$–V

2. Analyze the following passages by writing under each chord its appropriate Roman and Arabic numerals and above each nonharmonic tone its appropriate symbol.

    a. Mendelssohn — *Song Without Words, no. 16, op. 38, no. 4*

    b. Schumann — *Album for the Young, no. 9*

c. Schumann — *Carnaval, no. 11*

d. Schumann — *Album for the Young, no. 38, 1*

c : **THE** ii$_5^6$ **AND THE** vii$_{7b}^{o}$

The ii$_5^6$ has long been considered an enriched IV, a IV with an *added sixth*. It is, in fact, often called the "chord with the added sixth" (with the *sixte ajoutée*), a term first employed by Rameau. As such, the ii_5^6 is treated as wholly consonant, needing no special resolution, whether in Major or Minor.

The vii_7°, and more particularly the $vii_{7\flat}^\circ$, are further dominant harmonies which may replace the V in the cadence. They are, as some theorists call them, incomplete V_9 chords without their roots. A further peculiarity of the $vii_{7\flat}^\circ$ is that its inversions sound the same as the root position except for their pitch, since this chord divides the octave into four equal intervals (minor thirds). For this reason there exist only three different diminished seven-chords, except for enharmonic respellings.

The vii_7° and the $vii_{7\flat}^\circ$ deserve special attention because of their frequency.

EXERCISES

In the following exercises replace the IV by ii_5^6 and the forms of V_7 by the appropriate forms of vii_7° or $vii_{7\flat}^\circ$. Observe that $vii_{7(\flat)}^\circ$ may serve as an appoggiatura to, or a replacement of, V_5^6; $vii_{5(\flat)}^{\circ 6}$ is similarly related to V_3^4, and $vii_{3(\flat)}^{\circ 4}$ to V_2; but vii_2° serves best as an appoggiatura to V_7. Use nonharmonic tones in the soprano and transpose each exercise on the piano to at least two other keys.

1. E$\flat$ I–IV–V_7–vi–V_5^6–IV_4^6–I

2. f   i–VI–iv–V_2–i_6–ii_7°–V_3^4–$I_{4\ 3}^{5\ -}$†

3. G   I–V_3^4–I_6–IV–V_7–vi–V_5^6–I

4. a   i–iv–III_6^+–VI_7–ii_7°–V_5^6–iv_4^6–i

5. B   I–V_2–I_6–IV–V–V_3^4–$I_{4\ 3}^{5\ -}$†

6. c$\sharp$ i–iv_5^6–V_7††–i_6–iv–$i_4^{\cdot 6}$–V_3^4–i

d : SEQUENCES

Among the most favored devices of the late Baroque (c. 1680–1740) were fifth-fall progressions involving seven-chords. They were taught in the form of fifth-fall chains (see Chapter 12, section c(2)), each starting with a group of two chords which is repeated in a regularly

---

† This is a 4–3 suspension.

†† As in this instance, the resolution of the seventh in the progression from one seven-chord to another sometimes attracts so much attention that parallel fifths do not disturb and are permissible.

descending pattern as shown in the following exercises. Groups of tones or chords repeated in such a manner are called *sequences*.

In each of the following exercises the student must observe and fix in his mind the initial group of two chords. This group will be the "motif" of the sequence, and when the sequence is played on the piano, the fingering of this first group will be repeated with each repetition of the group on the various pitches.

EXERCISES

Write each exercise in one major and one minor key, and play each on the piano in these keys and in at least one additional major and minor key. In Minor the natural Minor is to be used except for the dominant harmony before the final tonic, which must employ the leading tone.

† In this sequence complete and incomplete seven-chords without fifths must be alternated.

14

APPENDIX TO PART II

a : RULES

(1) : Key-Signature Rules

(P. 40) When transposing a key a fifth up, add the one sharp or subtract the one flat in the key signature which modifies the subtonic of the new key. When transposing a fifth down, subtract the one sharp or add the one flat in the key signature which modifies the subdominant of the new key.

(P. 41) The flats and sharps in the key signatures of enharmonic keys always add up to twelve.

(P. 41) When ascending from a key to its chromatic neighbor, as from C Major to C-sharp Major, add seven accidentals in the key signature; when descending chromatically, subtract seven accidentals.

(P. 41) When ascending from a key to one a major second higher, add two accidentals in the key signature; when descending by a major second, subtract two accidentals.

(P. 43)   To find the key signature of a tonic Minor, subtract three accidentals from the key signature of the tonic Major.   To find the key signature of a tonic Major, add three accidentals to that of the tonic Minor.

(P. 43)   To find the tonic of a relative Minor, descend a minor third from the tonic of the relative Major.   To find the tonic of a relative Major, ascend a minor third from the relative Minor.

(P. 40-41)   To find the tonic of a piece of music, look at the initial and, particularly, the final cadence.   If it is in Major, the tonic is one step above the last sharp of the key signature or four steps down from the last flat.   If it is in Minor, go through the same process and then descend a minor third to find the tonic.

(2) : Part-Writing Rules

(P. 75-76)   When writing for four parts mostly in open harmony, place the soprano in the treble staff with stems up, the alto in the treble staff with stems down, the tenor in the bass staff with stems up, and the bass in the bass staff with stems down.   When writing mostly in close harmony, place the soprano as before, put the alto and tenor on a common downward stem in the treble staff, and the bass with stems up or down in the bass staff.

(P. 74)   Avoid consecutive primes, fifths, and octaves.

(P. 75)   A leading tone should not be doubled and must normally be led to the tonic (cf. p. 131).

(P. 151)   A stressed dissonant tone should not be left by leap.

(P. 124)   Sevenths and ninths should be neither reached in similar motion from an octave nor left in similar motion going to an octave when involving a skip in the soprano.

(P. 89)   Every nonharmonic tone must be heard as related to a chord tone on the same pitch or on one a single step away.

b : PROCEDURES AND SUGGESTIONS

(1) : Dictation Procedure

1. While listening to the melody, tap the strong beats with a foot and count them. This gives you the correct number of measures. Write the correct number of bar lines and observe whether the melody starts on a strong beat or an upbeat.

2. Continue tapping the strong beats with the foot, but also tap all beats with one hand and count how many there are in each measure. This gives the meter. Write down the meter signature.

3. Memorize the melody with the aid of motif and phrase repetitions.

4. Count the tones of the melody in each measure and write the number above each measure.

5. Distribute the tones in each measure among the beats.

6. Finally add the notes of correct pitch to this rhythmic scheme.

(2) : Harmonic Procedures

(P. 74)   To effect strict connections in root progressions by fourths:

1. Write the bass progression.

2. Complete the first chord.

3. Find the common tone and hold it in the same voice.

4. Lead the remaining voices stepwise to the nearest tones of the second chord.

(P. 85)   To effect strict connections in root progressions by seconds when only root-positioned chords are involved:

1. Write the bass progression.

2. Complete the first chord.

3. Lead all other voices to the nearest tones of the second chord in contrary motion to the bass.

(P. 115) To effect strict connections in root progressions by seconds when six-chords are involved:

1. Write the bass progression.

2. Complete the first chord.

3. Write the progression of the roots or that of the fifths in another part.

4. Lead one of the remaining voices (and, if possible, both of them) in contrary motion to the part just written.

(P. 91) When a melody is given:	When a bass is given:
1. Determine the implied harmonies.	1. Write out the soprano, using only chord tones.
2. Write out all bass tones with figures.	2. Add the middle parts.
3. Add the middle parts.	3. Add nonharmonic tones in the soprano and elsewhere.

(P. 103) To write a melody from a motif or phrase:

1. Clap the rhythm of the given motif or phrase and find a pleasing rhythm for the continuation, using some repetitions.

2. Add notes to the rhythmic scheme thus established with some melodic correspondences and consideration for the over-all contour.

(P. 126) When resolving a V_7:

1. Write the bass progression.

2. Lead the seventh stepwise down, or (more rarely) up, or hold it over.

3. Take the leading tone to the tonic, especially when in the soprano.

(Pp. 157,159) The ninth of the V_9 and the thirteenth of the V_7^{13} should always be in the soprano. The ninth resolves stepwise down or is held over, and the thirteenth resolves by a descent of a second or third, and, more rarely, by holding over.

Warnings

1. The complete V_7 will usually resolve to the incomplete I, and the incomplete V_7 to the complete I (p. 126).

2. When resolving to I_6, the seventh of the V_7, V_9, and V_7^{13} goes stepwise up.

3. In the deceptive cadence V–VI the third of VI will usually be doubled (p. 169).

(3) : Suggestions

1. Make melodies as interesting as possible by avoiding too many tone repetitions, especially when going from a weak beat to the succeeding strong one.

2. Avoid placing the harmony of a strong beat also on the preceding weak beat.

3. When the same harmony is heard twice in succession, this pause in harmonic movement should normally be used for melodic motion in the soprano.

4. When a melody tone is held or repeated, this pause in melodic movement should normally be used for a change of harmony.

5. The fewer harmonies used, the more clearly the melody will be heard, but too few harmonies result in boredom.

6. Do not normally use more harmonies per measure than there are beats.

7. In short melodies rarely use more than two skips, or one skip and two steps, or four steps in one direction, except when skipping through the tones of a triad.

8. To be pleasing and singable, a melody should rarely have a range of less than a sixth or more than an octave and a sixth.

9. Only once in the course of a melody should a highest tone, or climax, be reached. A single lowest tone, or anticlimax, is also desirable.

10. In general, no striking feature in a melody (such as an ornament, a characteristic interval, motif, or rhythm, or a peculiar harmonic progression) should occur only once, for it would stand out awkwardly or unreasonably.

III

CHROMATIC HARMONY AND MODULATION

15

STRICT DIATONIC MODULATION

(1) : The Three Main Operations

Modulation is the process of moving from one key to another. Each of the two keys must be firmly established by one or several cadences if modulation is to take place, and at first it will be best for the student to strengthen the cadence in the second key by using in it a I_4^6 and a V_7, V_9, or V_7^{13}, rather than a simple V triad.

The seemingly endless variety of possible modulations may be divided into two broad categories:

1. Modulations made with the help of a *modulator*, which connects the *first key* (the one from which we move) to the *second key* (the one to which we move)

2. Modulations achieved by *direct skip* from the first key to the second

There are always *three operations* in every modulation of the first category:

Op. 1. Establishment of the first key
Op. 2. Modulator (missing in modulations by skip)
Op. 3. Establishment of the second key

It is essential for the student to keep firmly in mind the two types of modulations and the three operations.

(2) : *Modulations by Skip*

Modulations by skip do not involve anything that has not been studied previously. After the cadence in the first key, the tonic or dominant of this key is simply followed (immediately or after a rest) by the tonic or another chord of the second key. This can be done (1) abruptly, by leap in one or several of the voices; (2) more smoothly, by stepwise or chromatic motion in all parts; or (3) by holding a tone in one part while the others move freely to the first chord of the second key. In all three cases the skip initiates a complete cadence in the second key, that is, a cadence which includes a subdominant, dominant, and tonic. The following examples will clarify these procedures:

EXERCISES

The student should improvise on the keyboard and then write out two of each type of modulation by skip, similar to those given in the preceding examples. Roughnesses will disappear if he remembers that the first chord of the second key need not be the tonic. Nonharmonic tones will also help.

(3) : *Types of Modulators*

In this and later chapters we are chiefly concerned with studying the various possible modulators used to bring about modulations which are not made by direct skip. These modulations fall into three general types: diatonic, chromatic, and enharmonic. The definitions of these three types of modulations must be committed to memory:

1. In *diatonic modulations* any two successive chords may be interpreted as belonging to the same key. Thus there is no tonal break at any point. The modulator consists of one or several chords which are common to both keys and which are called *pivot chords*.

2. In *chromatic modulations* there always is a place where two successive chords must be interpreted as belonging to different keys because one of the chords contains one or several notes present in the other chord but with different accidentals (such as F in one chord and F-sharp in the other). Thus there occurs at one point a tonal break between two chords, the second of which is the modulator. There is no pivot chord.

3. In *enharmonic modulations* there is always one chord which, through the enharmonic change of one or several (but not all) of its notes (such as C–E–G♯ and C–E–A♭), is interpreted as belonging to two keys. Thus there is at one point a tonal break within a single chord which functions as a pivot chord.

(4) : *Relative Majors and Minors*

Before dealing with diatonic modulation, let us agree that for present purposes *relative Majors and Minors are so closely related that no special modulation is necessary to go from one to the other.* Here, as in modulations by skip, operation 1 (the cadence of the first key) is immediately followed by operation 3 (the cadence of the second key). Such modulations are very frequent and will be used to good advantage.

EXERCISES

Write and play on the keyboard in two further keys modulations following the two given models:

1.

2. c   i–iv–V–i–   E♭   (I–)IV–I$_4^6$–V$_7$–I

As shown in the models, the second cadence should be made stronger by the use of I$_4^6$ and V$_7$ (or one of its derivatives). Otherwise employ any subdominant and dominant harmonies for IV and V. The steps enclosed in parentheses may be omitted at pleasure.

(5) : Direction and Degree of Modulations

The last preliminary to the study of diatonic modulation is the analysis of the direction and degree of modulations. Take any two Majors whose tonics are one fifth apart (such as C and G Major). In this instance C will be called the *lower Major* and G the *higher Major* because, when their tonics are at a distance of a fifth, C is the lower tone and G the higher. The lower of two such keys will always have one sharp less or one flat more in the key signature than the higher one. When modulations are made between two such keys, we shall speak of modulating one fifth, or *one harmonic degree*, up (from C to G) or one fifth, or one harmonic degree, down (from G to C). Since relative Majors and Minors have the same key signature, we shall speak not only of the modulation C–G as going one degree up (from no sharps to one sharp), but also of C–e, a–e, and a–G. Similarly, we speak of the modulations G–a, e–a, and e–C as going, like G–C, one degree down. It is essential that the student fix in his mind the direction between two keys — up or down — in the circle of fifths and the distance between them, best remembered as the difference of accidentals in the key signatures. To practice these relationships, answer this question in the following exercises: How many harmonic degrees, in which direction, separate the given pair of keys?

EXERCISES

1. D–E♭ (five degrees down: from two sharps to three flats)

2. f–b

3. A–g♯

4. B♭–b♭

5. c♯–F♯

6. g–F

7. B–e

8. a–c

b : TYPES OF FIRST-DEGREE MODULATIONS

Modulations up or down by one harmonic degree are called first-degree modulations. Of these, there are eight types, symbolized as follows:

1. M ⤴ M (from *Major* one degree up to Major), e. g., C–G

2. M ⤴ m (from *Major* one degree up to Minor), e. g., C–e

3. M ⤵ M (from Major one degree down to *Major*), e. g., G–C

4. m ⤵ M (from Minor one degree down to *Major*), e. g., e–C

5. m ⤴ M (from *Minor* one degree up to Major), e. g., a–G

6. m ⤴ m (from *Minor* one degree up to Minor), e. g., a–e

7. M ↘ m (from Major one degree down to *Minor*), e. g., G–a

8. m ↘ m (from Minor one degree down 'to *Minor*), e. g., e–a

The first four of these modulations involve the lower Major (italicized in the table) as either the first or second key, and the last four involve the lower Minor (also italicized). The significance of this difference will become clear in succeeding sections.

(1) : Pivot Chords

The problem in diatonic modulation is to find the appropriate pivot chords. The easiest way to do this for first-degree modulations is to compare the chords of four keys that may be involved (two Majors which are one harmonic degree apart and their relative Minors):

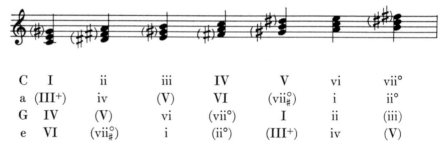

C	I	ii	iii	IV	V	vi	vii°
a	(III⁺)	iv	(V)	VI	(vii°♯)	i	ii°
G	IV	(V)	vi	(vii°)	I	ii	(iii)
e	VI	(vii°♯)	i	(ii°)	(III⁺)	iv	(V)

Any chord in parentheses employs one or two sharps; all other chords are common both to the particular key and to C Major. It is immediately evident that C I, iii, V, and vi also occur in G; three of these chords are also common to E Minor, but only one to A Minor. There would, of course, be more common chords in the Minors if we used the chords of the natural Minor, which are identical with those of the relative Major. For the purposes of strict diatonic modulation, however, only the harmonic Minor will be considered.

(2) : Group 1, Involving the Lower Major

To make it easier to remember our modulators, we shall always think of *pivot chords as chords of the lower Major*. In first-degree modulations that involve the lower Major (which is C Major in the preceding table)

as either the first or the second key, the following pivot chords may be used:

M ✗ M: I, iii, V, vi of the lower Major

M ✗ m: I, iii, vi of the lower Major

M ↖ M: I, iii, V, vi of the lower Major

m ↖ M: I, iii, vi of the lower Major

(3) : Symbols

The student should use the following symbols in all written modulations. Using them will greatly facilitate his understanding of the procedure involved. These symbols are:

1. The staggering of lines, so that one line is reserved for each key or for each pair of relative Major and Minor.

2. The vertical alignment of the two interpretations of the pivot chords.

3. Brackets marking operations 1 and 3, and a circle for operation 2 (the modulator).

(4) : Standard First-Degree Pivots

Observe the use of these symbols in the following exercises, in which each of the pivot chords which may be used in M ✗ M modulations is applied in turn.

EXERCISES

1. Write out each exercise. Then play it on the piano and transpose it a fifth up.

op. 1

a. A♭ I–IV–V*–I
 E♭ IV–I$_4^6$–V$_7$–I

op. 3

op. 1

b. B   I–IV–V*–I*–iii

F♯   vi–IV*–I$_4^6$–V$_7$–I

op. 3

op. 1

c. G   I–IV–V*–I*–V

D   I–IV*–I$_4^6$–V$_7$–I

op. 3

op. 1

d. B♭   I–IV–V*(–I*)–vi

F   ii–I$_4^6$–V$_7$–I

op. 3

Close inspection shows that the pivot chords iii and V used in exercises b and c are unnecessary; the chords marked "*" are all also possible pivots. In fact, in exercise b the progression I–iii is awkward, and in exercise c the repetition V–I–V is disturbing. Only exercises a and d sound smooth. We may therefore conclude that the best and fastest M ⚹ M modulations are by way of I or vi of the lower Major, and that the presence of two successive pivot chords assures smoothness, provided by V* in exercises a and d. To be sure, V may not be available if another dominant is used in the first key. Therefore, the best two-chord modulator in M ⚹ M modulations will be *I–vi of the lower Major*.

2. In the following exercises each of the pivot chords which may be used in M ⚹ m modulations is applied in turn. Write out each exercise. Then play it on the piano and transpose it a fifth up.

op. 1

a. D I–IV–V–(I)(–vi)

f♯ (VI)–iv*–i⁴₄–V₇–i

op. 3

op. 1

b. G♭ I–IV–V–I*–(iii)(–vi)

b♭ (i)–iv*–i⁴₄–V₇–i

op. 3

op. 1

c. E I–IV–V–I*–(vi)

g♯ (iv)–I⁴₄–V₇–i

op. 3

Exercises a and c are identical except for the keys chosen here, and exercise b merely adds an extra, unnecessary chord to the same progression, I–vi of the first key. Consequently, M ↗m, like M ↗M, best uses I–vi (of the lower Major) as pivot chords.

3. Write out and play M ↖M and m ↖M modulations as done in exercises 1 and 2, by using in turn each possible pivot.

Doing this will show the student that, as with the two types of modulations discussed in the preceding exercises, these modulations can be made smooth and efficient by a single general procedure: the use of the double pivot *I–vi of the lower Major* (in this order because chord progressions by a third down are better than those by a third up). Although I alone will suffice in some of these modulations, vi will never be awkward and will often be necessary.

(5) : Group 2, Involving the Lower Minor

Because of its leading tone, the lower Minor has only one chord in common with either of the keys which are one harmonic degree higher. Since two pivot chords are needed to make most modulations smooth, first-degree modulations from and to the lower Minor often employ its relative Major (the lower Major) as an intermediary. In this way the disturbing leading tone disappears (for instance, the G-sharp of A Minor disappears in C Major) and the pivot chords of the lower Major become available. The following table of operations will clarify the procedure:

	m ⤴ M and m ⤴ m	M ⤵ m and m ⤵ m
Op. 1.	Cadence of first key	Cadence of first key
Op. 1a.	Tonic chord of lower Major	
Op. 2.	Pivot chords (I–vi)	Pivot chords (I–vi)
Op. 2a.		Cadence of lower Major
Op. 3.	Cadence of second key	Cadence of second key

When the lower Minor is the *first* key, operation *1a* is inserted (consisting of the single tonic triad of the lower Major). When the lower Minor is the *second* key, operation *2a* is inserted (consisting of a complete or a deceptive cadence in the lower Major). The basic three operations remain as before, as do the pivot chords: I–vi of the lower Major.

The following exercises will show the general procedure. The student should, however, construct (with symbols) and write out (in musical notation) one exercise of each of the four types (m ⤴ M, m ⤴ m, M ⤵ m, and m ⤵ m), each starting in another key. Then play these exercises on the piano and transpose them down by a major third.

EXERCISES

1. m ⤴ m: d   i–iv–V–i – F   I–vi

_{op. 1   op. 1a}

a   VI–iv–i$^6_4$–V$_7$–i

_{op. 3}

op. 1

2. M ♮ m: A   I–IV–V–I*–(IV–ii)

D   I–vi–IV–I$_4^6$–V$_7$(–I) — b   i–iv–i$_4^6$–V$_7$–i

op. 2a   op. 3

(Note that a single line is used for relative Majors and Minors.)

(6) : Summary

Although the type of modulator we have been studying is but one of several possible modulators, it is the most generally applicable and the smoothest. I–vi of the lower Major provides the easiest method of first-degree modulation, since the student must remember only four rules, which cover all eight types of such modulations:

1. Determine the harmonic degree (distance in the circle of fifths) and the direction of the modulation (up or down).

2. Employ the three main operations, the second (pivot chords) being I–vi of the lower Major.

3. Use either of the two auxiliary operations (1a or 2a) when the lower Minor is involved.

4. Employ I$_4^6$ and V$_7$ in the cadences of operations 2a and 3.

The analysis of a Bach chorale (*Ermuntre dich*, BR 102) will clarify the use of such strict diatonic modulations:

G I   I   I

D IV V   I   IV

EXERCISES

Write out the following exercises in symbols only and play them on the piano. Modulate from:

1. F to g

2. E♭ to B♭

3. f to b♭

4. D♭ to G♭

5. f♯ to c♯

6. b to G

7. F♯ to a♯

8. e♭ to D♭

c : SECOND-DEGREE MODULATIONS

After first-degree modulation, the next step in strict diatonic modulation is *second-degree modulation*, which is modulation between two

Majors or their relative Minors which are two fifths apart along the circle of fifths and which have key signatures differing by two sharps, two flats, or one sharp and one flat. The types of second-degree modulations are completely identical with the eight types of first-degree modulations, as are the three main operations and the two auxiliary operations 1a and 2a, which are employed when the lower Minor is involved as the first or second key. The only difference between first- and second-degree modulations concerns operation 2: the pivot chords.

Again, the best way to find which pivot chords to use is to compare four keys which may be involved (two Majors which are two harmonic degrees apart and their relative Minors):

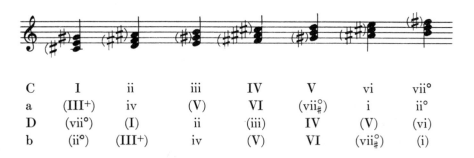

C	I	ii	iii	IV	V	vi	vii°
a	(III⁺)	iv	(V)	VI	(vii°♯)	i	ii°
D	(vii°)	(I)	ii	(iii)	IV	(V)	(vi)
b	(ii°)	(III⁺)	iv	(V)	VI	(vii°♯)	(i)

Clearly C iii and V are the only chords that also occur in D Major and B Minor, whereas A Minor shares no chords with the higher keys and therefore must rely on its relative Major for pivot chords (involving operations 1a or 2a). In first-degree modulations the pivot chords were I, iii, V, and vi of the lower Major, and of these four chords the most important were I and vi. In second-degree modulations only the other two chords — iii and V — are satisfactory.† Since two pivots are needed for smooth modulation, we shall use both chords in every second-degree modulation. Because a group of chords descending by thirds is more pleasing than an ascending group, the pivot chords will be *V–iii of the lower Major* rather than iii–V.

A few exercises will suffice.

---

† The two sets of pivot chords for first- and second-degree modulations may also be remembered as a single one: IV–ii of the higher Major. However, the symbols as set forth here serve the memory better.

EXERCISES

1. Write out each exercise, play it on the piano, and transpose it up by a major third.

op. 1

a. M ℳ M: F   I–IV(–V–I)–V–iii

G   IV–ii –I$_4^6$–V$_7$–I

op. 3

op. 1

b. m ℳ M: c   i–iv–V–i–VI–iv

D♭   V–iii –ii$_6$–I$_4^6$–V$_7$–I

op. 3

op. 1   op. 1a

c. m ℳ m: b   i–iv–V–i — D   I–V–iii

c♯   VI–iv –i$_4^{\cdot 6}$–V$_7$–i

op. 3

op. 1

d. M ℳ m: A♭   I–IV–V–I–IV–ii

G♭   V–iii –ii$_6$–I$_4^6$–V$_7$(–I) — e♭   i–iv–i$_4^{\cdot 6}$–V$_7$–i

op. 2a   op. 3

2. Construct the following exercises in symbols only.   Then play each on the piano and transpose it to two other keys.   Modulate from:

a. D to c♯   **c.** f♯ to B

b. F to E♭   **d.** g to f

d : MODULATIONS BY THREE TO SIX DEGREES

A comparison of the chords of two pairs of relative Majors and Minors at a distance of three or more fifths will show the student that such keys do not have any common chords which may serve as pivots. Consequently, it is impossible to achieve strict diatonic modulation between keys more than two harmonic degrees apart. These more distant modulations must be made as double or triple modulations. For example, a fourth-degree modulation, such as from E Major to F Minor, is achieved through two second-degree modulations: either E to F♯ (G♭) to f or E to d♯ (e♭) to f. There are even four possible routes for a third-degree modulation such as from g to G: g–d–G, g–F–G, g–a–G, or g–C–G. In such double modulations the second key becomes a *pivot key* to the third, and operation 3 of the first modulation (the cadence in the second key) serves as operation 1 of the second modulation. Exercise 1, which follows, will suffice to clarify the principle.

While double modulation is sometimes desirable to permit greater expansion of a composition, it may often be merely cumbersome. Therefore, when faster modulation to distant keys is needed, one often turns to modal mixtures (see next chapter), which extend the possibilities of diatonic modulation by offering many additional pivot chords. The longest strictly diatonic modulations ever necessary are triple modulations by five or six harmonic degrees up or down, reaching half around the circle of fifths.

EXERCISES

1. Write out and play the following exercise and transpose it a minor third up:

In order to save space, the same exercise may be written with the symbols staggered as follows:

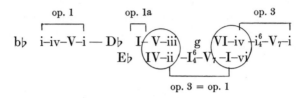

2. Construct, write out, play, and transpose by a minor third up the following modulations:

    a. A♭–c♯ (use enharmonic change)   **b.** d–G♭

16

MODAL MIXTURES

Modal mixtures may be defined as the *use in a key of tones from other modal scales based on the same tonic.* They constitute the first important source of chromaticism, that is, of the use of tones outside the diatonic scale. These mixtures are most characteristic of nineteenth-century style, but ever since Major and Minor emerged in the seventeenth century as the main modes of Western music, tones of the one mode have been introduced in compositions following the other mode.

(1) : Relative and Tonic Majors and Minors

Mixtures of relative and of tonic Majors and Minors have always been especially frequent. In compositions that exploit relative Majors and Minors, the tonality shifts between that of the main key and that of its relative (for example, between C Major and A Minor). This procedure leads to a variety of attractive secondary cadences, but not to much chromaticism. On the other hand, many colorful and interesting chromaticisms are produced by the introduction of the third, sixth, or seventh step of a Minor into its tonic Major (for example, of the E♭, A♭, or B♭ of C Minor into C Major) and vice versa. Some of these mixtures between tonic Majors and Minors are very common, for those variants of Minor known as "harmonic" and "melodic" are simply the results of introducing steps of a Major into its tonic Minor. In one the seventh step and in the other the sixth and seventh steps of a Minor are replaced by those of its tonic Major.

(2) : The Phrygian Second

The second step in Minor is another result of the influence of Major. Obviously, the minor second is more characteristic of Minor, for with a minor second the minor scale forms only minor and perfect intervals between the tonic and the other scale steps, just as the major scale forms only major and perfect intervals. Also, the minor scale with the minor second is the exact inversion of the major scale:

		1		1		$\frac{1}{2}$		1		1		1		$\frac{1}{2}$		(1 = whole tone;
Major:	C		D		E		F		G		A		B		C	$\frac{1}{2}$ = half tone)
Minor:	C		B♭		A♭		G		F		E♭		D♭		C	

One of the Medieval or Church modes, the Phrygian, was constructed like this minor scale, with a minor second, but the craving for the leading tone and its introduction from Major finally led to the modification of this second step so that two consecutive half-tone steps might be avoided (in C, for example: B♮–C–D♭). Nevertheless, the Phrygian minor second is still frequently used in both Minor and Major. Similarly, admixtures from the other Church modes affect Major and Minor. We must therefore turn briefly to these modes.

(3) : The Church Modes

The six main modes of Western music are shown in the following table. The first group contains the three modes which are characterized by a minor third; the second, those which are characterized by a major third:

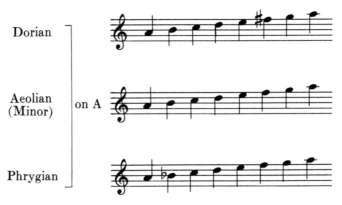

Dorian

Aeolian (Minor)   on A

Phrygian

Usually these modes are presented as white-key scales in the following order: Ionian (on C), Dorian (on D), Phrygian (on E), Lydian (on F), Mixolydian (on G), and Aeolian (on A). But, like Major and Minor, each of these modes may be transposed to any tonic, so that we can have, for example, E♭ Dorian, E♭ Phrygian, E♭ Lydian, or E♭ Mixolydian, as well as E♭ Major and E♭ Minor.

As the table shows, the Dorian mode differs from Minor in only one step: the major sixth, which is the outstanding characteristic of the Dorian mode. Accordingly, we speak of the *Dorian sixth* in Minor (particularly when it occurs together with the minor seventh; otherwise it is more easily understood as the usual *major sixth* of the "melodic" Minor). The key signature of A Dorian is, because of the major sixth, one sharp (F♯) as compared with no sharps in A Minor. Similarly, E Dorian has two sharps as opposed to E Minor's one, E♭ Dorian has five flats as opposed to E♭ Minor's six, and so on. In other words, any Dorian key will have one sharp more or one flat less in the key signature than its tonic Minor.†

Conversely, A Phrygian has a key signature of one flat, and any Phrygian key has one flat more or one sharp less in the key signature than its tonic Minor. The Phrygian second, the characteristic interval of the mode, accounts for the difference in key signature.

Lydian is related to Major as Dorian is to Minor, having one sharp more or one flat less in the key signature than its tonic Major.

† Examples of such key signatures are found in BR, numbers 8, 15, 19, 25, 49, 66, and 87, to name but a few. It should be noted, however, that despite these signatures Bach's harmonizations normally employ pure Major or Minor.

Its characteristic interval is the augmented fourth, called the *Lydian fourth*.

Mixolydian is related to Major as Phrygian is to Minor, having one flat more or one sharp less than its tonic Major, from which it deviates by a minor seventh, known as the *Mixolydian seventh* (called *Aeolian seventh* in Minor).

The following table provides a summary of the preceding discussion:

Mode	*Key signature*	*Characteristic step*
Dorian:	1 sharp more or 1 flat less than Minor	major sixth (in Minor)
Phrygian:	1 sharp less or 1 flat more than Minor	minor second
Lydian:	1 sharp more or 1 flat less than Major	augmented fourth
Mixolydian:	1 sharp less or 1 flat more than Major	minor seventh (in Major)

EXERCISES

1. a. Write the key signatures of B♭ Dorian, Phrygian, Lydian, and Mixolydian.

b. Write the key signatures of C♯ Dorian, Phrygian, Lydian, and Mixolydian.

2. a. Write the Dorian sixth, Phrygian second, Lydian fourth, and Aeolian seventh in B Minor and E♭ Minor.

b. Write the Phrygian second, Lydian fourth, and Mixolydian seventh in F♯ Major and A♭ Major.

3. a. Play the E♭ Major, E♭ Lydian, and E♭ Mixolydian scales. Then play the E♭ Minor, E♭ Dorian, and E♭ Phrygian scales.

b. Do the same on the tonic B♭.

b : PRIMARY MIXTURES

Just as the steps of a major scale may replace the normal steps in its
tonic Minor, and vice versa, so the steps of the tonic Dorian, Phrygian,
Lydian, or Mixolydian may be introduced into either the tonic Minor
or Major, the result being chromaticism. For example, C Major may
contain the following tones:

C, D♭(Ph)†, D, E♭(m), E, F, F♯(L), G, A♭(m), A, B♭(Mix), B

Similarly, C Minor may contain the very same tones:

C, D♭(Ph), D, E♭, E(M), F, F♯(L), G, A♭, A(D,M), B♭(Ae), B(M)

Theoretically, therefore, the same triads are possible in either Major
or Minor, but in practice certain mixtures are more important than
others.

(1) : Subdominants

The most frequent mixtures between different modes occur on *subdominant chords*.

(a) : In Major

In C Major the following chromatically altered subdominants occur:

1. A minor triad on the fourth step (iv): the *minor subdominant*, often
called "minor-major" subdominant, that is, Minor-derived instead of
Major-derived subdominant

† The abbreviations are: Ae = Aeolian, D = Dorian, L = Lydian, M = Major, m = Minor,
Mix = Mixolydian, Ph = Phrygian. They indicate the mode from which a tone is derived.

2. A major triad on the lowered sixth step (VI♭): the *minor submediant,* that is, Minor-derived submediant which, despite its name, is a major triad

3. A diminished triad on the second step with or without a seventh (ii° or ii⁷₀): the *minor supertonic*

4. A major triad on the lowered second step (II♭): the *Phrygian supertonic,* whose first inversion is called the *Neapolitan six-chord,*† symbolized *N6* (see next section)

5. A major triad on the second step (II): the *Lydian supertonic* (used more rarely)

(b) : In Minor

Chromatic subdominants in C Minor are:

6. A major triad on the fourth step (IV): the *major subdominant,* also called "major-minor," that is, Major-derived subdominant

7. A minor triad on the raised sixth step (vi♯): the *major (or Dorian) submediant*

8. A minor triad on the second step (ii): the *major (or Dorian) supertonic*

9. A major triad on the lowered second step (II♭): the *Phrygian supertonic,* and its first inversion, the *Neapolitan six-chord* (see next section)

† So named because it was once believed to have been first employed by a group of eighteenth-century opera composers in Naples, Italy.

EXERCISES

1. Write and play the cadence I–IV–I$_4^6$–V$_7$–I in D Major and D Minor, and replace IV successively by the nine mixtures listed in the preceding section.

2. Do the same in F♯ Major and F♯ Minor.

(2) : *The Neapolitan Six-Chord*

The following three examples show some of the uses of modal mixtures, each of which is indicated by a "*":

Dvořák — *Slavonic Dance, op. 72, no. 16*

Beethoven — *Piano Sonata no. 17, op. 31, no. 2, third movement*

Schubert — *String Quartet Movement in C Minor, op. posth.*

The last two examples include a Phrygian triad and a Neapolitan six-chord. A Neapolitan six-chord may be easily constructed if it is considered as the first inversion of a major triad on the lowered supertonic (the Phrygian triad). This chord is a major six-chord with the subdominant in the bass; it is therefore heard as a subdominant chord and may be used wherever a IV can be used. Consequently, the bass tone of the Neapolitan six-chord is usually doubled. Its sixth normally progresses to the tonic (as part of I, IV, or VI), or it descends by a *diminished third* to the leading tone (as part of V or VII). This diminished third is highly characteristic of progressions involving the Neapolitan six-chord and must be carefully practiced.

EXERCISES

Write and play the cadences I–II♭₆–V₇–I and I–II♭₆–V₇¹³–I, each in two major and two minor keys.

(3) : The Picardy Third

Modal mixtures in the tonic triad are, of course, rare, because they destroy the distinction between Major and Minor. Nevertheless, because of a Medieval notion that the minor triad was less consonant than the major triad, composers of the seventeenth and eighteenth centuries often gave compositions in Minor a final tonic triad with a major third, the so-called *Picardy third*.† And since the early nineteenth century, major and minor triads with the same root have often been contrasted within a phrase for particular effects.

(4) : Other Mixtures

A number of other modal mixtures may also be used. In C Major and C Minor these mixtures are:

10. The minor triad on the fifth step (v), the *minor dominant*, is rare in either Major or Minor. It always evokes a quality of antiquity or of church music.

11. The *minor* (-derived) *mediant* in Major (III♭) and the *major* (-derived) *mediant* in Minor (iii♯) are more frequent and very colorful.

12. The *Aeolian* and *Mixolydian subtonics* (VII♭) are equally frequent and colorful.

13. The minor triad on the leading tone, the *Lydian subtonic*, is rather rare, on the other hand.

14. One of the most frequent mixtures is the *diminished seven-chord* (vii°₇♭) in Major.

† Picardy is a northwestern province of France, but this geographic reference implies nothing. Examples of endings with a Picardy third are found, for example, in BR, numbers 8, 12, 13, 15, 17, 19, 23, 25, and 28.

EXERCISES

1. a. Write and play the following cadence in G Major and G Minor. Then replace V, III, and VII by mixtures 10, 11, and 12–14 respectively, and use the Picardy third in Minor: I–V–III–VI–IV–VII–V$_7$–I.

   b. Do the same in E Major and E Minor.

2. Asterisks indicate modal mixtures in the following exercises, which are to be written out in four parts, then played on the piano and transposed a major second up. In every case the chromatic (or "altered") chord must be constructed so that it can be explained as a substitution from another mode with the same tonic. When a progression sounds too sudden or surprising, a few nonharmonic tones, particularly suspensions and appoggiaturas, will improve the sound greatly.

   c. B   I–vi–II$_6$*–V–iii$_7$–II$_{♮6}^6$–I$_4^6$–vii$_{5♮}^{°6}$*–IV$_4^6$–I

   d. E♭   I–vi–VII$_♭$*–v*–III$_♭$*–iv*–ii–I$_4^6$–V$_7$–iv$_4^6$*–I

3. Several examples from the literature follow, each including some modal mixtures. These examples should be harmonized with simple chords. Playing them over on the piano, the student may dissolve these chords into various broken-chord accompaniment motifs, each retained throughout an example. Finally, the student should compare his solutions with the original settings.

   a. Schubert — *Die liebe Farbe (Die schöne Müllerin, no. 16)*

b. Schubert — *Der Müller und der Bach (Die schöne Müllerin, no. 19)*

c. Schubert — *Die Krähe (Winterreise, no. 15, end)*

d. Brahms — *Sommerabend*

e. Brahms — *Wie Melodien zieht es mir*

f. Brahms — *Die Spröde*

g. Mahler — *Lied des Verfolgten im Turm (measures 67-70)*

4. The composition of short phrases, aided by the use of mixtures and non-harmonic tones, will do much to develop the student's technique.

c : SECONDARY MIXTURES

We have been concerned with what may be called "primary modal mixtures," but there are others — *secondary mixtures* — which are simply substitutions of a major for a minor triad (or seven-chord), or vice versa, on any step of a scale. While such substitutions are quite frequent and colorful, they should be used only rarely by the student at this stage, because they do not refer to any mode and are therefore confusing. Most of these substitutions and their uses must wait for better explanations in later chapters.

In general, a cadence will sound satisfactory as long as the bass marks the main functions, whatever the modifications in the other parts may be. For example, the bass progression I–IV–V–I will produce an effective cadence, even if the chords above it are strongly modified.　In the following examples a single asterisk marks primary mixtures, and a double asterisk indicates secondary ones.

Reger — *Capriccio in C, op. 44, no. 10 (measures 11-12)*

Liszt — *Liebestraum no. 1*

Dvořák — *Symphony no. 5, second movement*

17

EXTENDED DIATONIC MODULATION

Modulation using modal mixtures does not differ essentially from strict diatonic modulation. In both kinds of modulation the three basic operations are fundamental, and the problem is still to find pivot chords through which the desired key may be reached. Modal mixtures merely open up new and more colorful possibilities. Therefore, modulation using modal mixtures may be called *extended diatonic* modulation.

In the most distant strictly diatonic modulation, such as that from C Major or A Minor to D Major or B Minor, only the following pivot chords can be used:

C	iii, V
a	- -
D	ii, IV
b	iv, VI

However, modal mixtures provide many additional pivots, as may be seen in the following table, which includes only the most usual mixtures:

C:	I		IIIb	iii		IV	v	V	vi	VIIb	vii
a:	III	IV		v	V	VI		VII♮	i	IIb	ii
D:	VII♮	I	IIb	ii		III♮	iv	IV	v	VIb	vi
b:	II♮	III		iv	IV			VI	VII♮		i

Although two or three separate strictly diatonic modulations are
necessary in modulations to distant keys, the mixtures provide numerous quick avenues through direct pivots (which may have to be enharmonically spelled). For example, in the modulation from C Major to
G-flat Major or E-flat Minor, mixtures provide the following pivot
chords:

C:	i		IIb	iv	v	V	VIb	VIIb	vii
Gb:			V	vii		IIbb			iv
eb:		vi♮	VIIb	ii	iii♮		IV	V	

The variety of possibilities offered by modal mixtures is rather
bewildering at first. The student must first become familiar with all
possible chords in modally mixed keys. As was shown in the preceding
chapter, the following triads can be used (and sevenths may be added
to any of them) in any mixed key, whether Major or Minor:

I, i
IIb, II, ii, ii°
IIIb, III$_b^+$, iii, iii°
IV, iv, iv$_{\sharp}^{\circ}$
V, v
VIb, vi, vi°
VIIb, viib, vii, vii°

A mere scanning of these chords in the first key of a modulation will reveal the ones which also belong to the second key and which may function as pivots. We must concentrate here on a few of the most frequently used and most effective pivot chords of this type. Once these standard modulators of extended diatonic modulation are mastered, the others may be easily employed for variety, and the inquisitive student will want to experiment with all of them.

EXERCISES

In the following modulations use in turn for pivot chords all possible mixtures listed in the preceding paragraph.

1. Modulate from B♭ to c♯. Here, for instance, B♭ iv may be used as c♯ ii, B♭ VI♭ as c♯ IV, and B♭ VII♭ as c♯ V. Construct, write out, and play each of these modulations.

2. Modulate from f♯ to E♭.

While fruitful for experimentation, these exercises will convince the student that clearer, more definite procedures are desirable, to which we now proceed.

b : STANDARD PIVOTS

(1) : Substitution of Major for Minor and Vice Versa

One of the simplest ways to modulate is to substitute a tonic Major for a prevailing Minor, or vice versa. This may be done by substituting the major triad on the tonic for the expected minor triad at the end of a cadence (Picardy third) or by merely changing the third of the tonic triad. For example, after landing on the expected major triad on the tonic, its third may be altered chromatically downward. These two procedures are illustrated by the following examples:

Schubert — *Wanderer Fantasy, third movement (measures 127–131)*

Beethoven — *Piano Sonata no. 16, op. 31, no. 1, second movement (measures 31–35)*

Schubert — *Piano Sonata in G, op. 78, second movement (measures 107–113)*

Such substitutions always produce a shift by three fifths in the circle of fifths, thereby making available pivots to keys three and four fifths away. In such modulations to keys *higher* in the circle of fifths, a tonic Major is substituted for a Minor. For example, in D Minor the substitute major triad on the tonic equals D I, b III, A IV, or f♯ VI. When the first key is a Major, go first to the relative Minor and then substitute *its* tonic Major. Starting in F Major, for example, go to D Minor and then substitute D I at the end of the cadence. In modulations to keys *lower* in the circle of fifths, a tonic Minor is substituted for a Major. For example, the tonic triad in G Major will be changed to a minor triad, which equals g i, B♭ vi, F ii, d iv, or E♭ iii. When the first key is a Minor, go first to the relative Major and then substitute *its* tonic Minor. Starting in E Minor, for example, go to G Major and then end that cadence with a minor triad on the tonic.

EXERCISES

With the aid of such Major-Minor substitutions modulate on the piano from:

1. F to A♭   **3.** b to g♯

2. g to e   **4.** D♭ to B♭

(2) : Modulation through the Neapolitan Six-Chord

One of the most helpful pivot chords for distant modulations is the *Neapolitan six-chord of the second key* (that of the first key being much less good). It must be remembered that any major triad in the first key can function in the second key as a Phrygian triad (which is the root position of the Neapolitan six-chord, built on the lowered super-tonic). Thus in modulating from C Major:

C I_6 can act as N6 of B or b, a distance of five or two degrees up
C IV_6 can act as N6 of E or e, a distance of four or one degrees up
C V_6 can act as N6 of F♯ or f♯, a distance of six or three degrees up

Likewise, in modulating from A Minor:

a III_6 can act as N6 of B or b, a distance of five or two degrees up
a V_6 can act as N6 of D♯ or d♯, a distance of nine or six degrees up
a VI_6 can act as N6 of E or e, a distance of four or one degrees up
a VII_6 can act as N6 of F♯ or f♯, a distance of six or three degrees up

In general, any major triad may be used as a pivot chord to the major or minor key with a tonic which is a half-tone below the root of that major triad. It is best to use only strictly diatonic major triads in the first key, because a double mixture is difficult for the listener to follow.

Modulations by way of the Neapolitan six-chord of the second key thus cover from one to six harmonic degrees ascending in the circle of fifths, and in one instance even nine degrees (or three down). This chord is therefore very useful for moving half way around the circle of fifths, five or six degrees, in one smooth and quick modulation. Direction loses significance here, since ascent and descent by six degrees from any point on the circle arrive at the same spot.   Nevertheless, such modulations are always heard as ascending.   An enharmonic interpretation of the second key is, of course, always possible in the modulation.

The following example will clarify the procedure:

op. 1

$$g \quad i–iv–V–i \underbrace{V_6}_{D\flat \quad N6}–I_4^6–V_7–I$$

op. 3

Since here only one pivot chord occurs, an additional chord of transition is often desirable.   In the example, g V_6 may be preceded by g V, or within the g V_6 the usual doubling of the root or fifth may be followed by that of the third, which is characteristic of the Neapolitan six-chord:

op. 1

$$g \quad i–iv–V–i–\underbrace{V–V_6}_{D\flat \quad N6}–I_4^6–V_7–I$$

op. 3

or

op. 1

$$g \quad i–iv–V–i–\underbrace{V_6^6 \ (or\ V_6^{10})–V_6^8}_{D\flat \quad N6}–I_4^6–V_7–I$$

op. 3

EXERCISES

With the aid of the Neapolitan six-chord modulate on the piano from:

1. A to D♭   3. G♭ to f   5. B to F

2. d to g♯   4. f♯ to C   6. c to D

(3) : Modulation through iv and VI♭ in Major

Further usual pivots are the Minor-derived subdominant and sub-mediant in Major. (Major subdominants and submediants in Minor are less efficient.) These pivots are usually *chords of the first key* or of the relative Major of the first key, although they may be used as chords of the second key. They make possible modulation from three to five degrees downward in the circle of fifths. For example, the F Minor and A♭ Major harmonies easily lead from C (or from A Minor via C) to E♭, A♭, f, and D♭ (but not so directly to b♭). Here is a typical example:

EXERCISES

With the aid of iv and VI♭ in Major, modulate on the piano from:

1. E to F   3. A♭ to E

2. g to D♭   4. g♯ to e

c : SUMMARY

The three standard pivots of extended diatonic modulation are:

1. Substitution of tonic Major for Minor, leading 3–4 degrees up
   Substitution of tonic Minor for Major, leading 3–4 degrees down

2. The N6 of the second key, usually leading 4–6 degrees up

3. The Minor-derived iv or VI♭ in Major in the first key, leading 3–5 degrees down.

In order to become proficient in this nearly inexhaustible field, the student is urged to construct for himself various problems similar to those in the following exercises. Some of these modulations will sound rather strained and farfetched, but smooth voice leading, a chromatic passing tone here and there, and a melodic main voice will improve the situation in every case. It must be kept in mind that we are here studying mere skeletons of music which need the flesh of polyphony and the blood of rhythmic-melodic flow in order to come alive as music. The more abrupt some chord connections sound, the more time must be consumed on each chord by melodic-contrapuntal means, so that the connection may be more thoroughly grasped.

EXERCISES

1. Construct, write out, and play each of the following exercises. Modulate with the aid of the N6 or the minor iv and VI♭ of Major from:

   a. A♭ to G   **c.** F♯ to D

   b. f to B   **d.** B♭ to C♭

2. Construct a table similar to those given in section a for each of the following exercises. Then use in turn all possible pivot chords to modulate from:

   a. A (or a) to B and g♯

   b. E (or e) to B♭ and g

   c. C (or c) to A♭ and f

Each exercise is to be constructed, written out, played, and transposed on the piano by a whole tone down.

18

SECONDARY DOMINANTS AND

CHROMATIC MEDIANTS

a : SECONDARY DOMINANTS

Secondary dominants may be defined as dominants of *any harmony of a key other than the tonic*. They provide the second important source of "altered chords." Since J. S. Bach (1685–1750) excelled in the use of secondary dominants, let us study a few examples from his music:

Herzliebster Jesu (BR 105)

* iv * V

Herzlich lieb hab' ich dich   (BR 107, end)

Schwing dich auf   (BR 142, middle)

(1) : Tonicization

In the preceding examples the diatonic harmonies are indicated in order to clarify the harmonic plan of the cadence. The secondary dominants, which are marked by asterisks, do not belong to the key of the particular example. Instead, they are dominant chords which lead to other tonics, tonics that are also harmonies of the main key. Thus in the first example (which is in B Minor) the first chord is a V_5^6 of E Minor (that is, of b iv) and the third chord a $vii_{7\flat}^\circ$ of F♯ Major (that is, of b V). The symbols for these chords are V_5^6/iv and $vii_{7\flat}^\circ/V$ respectively. These chromatic chords do not alter the regular ground plan of the cadence, but they enrich it through strengthening the various harmonies of the cadence, by leading into them as though they were tonics, a procedure we shall call *tonicization*, or *tonicizing*.

The secondary dominants shown in the preceding examples function as dominants of the various cadence harmonies because of the leading tones they contain.   These chords move exactly like normal dominants: their sevenths, ninths, and leading tones must be treated according to the rules of the V_7 chord and its relatives.   These chromatic chords are called secondary dominants in order to distinguish them from the diatonic dominants.

In order to construct a secondary dominant, one must think of the harmony that is tonicized as temporarily representing a tonic (of another key) and use all the accidentals that belong to the key represented by this tonic.   Thus in the first of the preceding examples the first two chords "belong" to E Minor and involve a D$\sharp$, and the next two chords "belong" to F$\sharp$ Major and therefore involve G$\sharp$ and E$\sharp$.   Any dominant chord can serve as a secondary dominant: V, V_7, V_9, V_7^{13}, vii$_7^\circ$, vii$_7^\circ\flat$, vii$^\circ$, III$^+$, and all their inversions.   The simple V triad, however, is usually too weak.

(2) : The Second Dominant

The most frequent secondary dominant is the dominant of V (D/V), known as the *second dominant*.   (Its dominant is sometimes called the "third dominant.")   An instance of the second dominant is provided in the last of the preceding musical illustrations, where the phrase closes with a half-cadence on V_6/v (V_6 of A Minor, the minor dominant of D Minor), and the next phrase starts logically with v.   The second dominant often replaces the subdominant in the cadence, and a second dominant may be followed by any form of V — not only by a V triad, but also by a V_7, a V_9, or any of their inversions.   A I_4^6 may also follow a second dominant.   In the progression D/V–V–I it is usual to include a seventh in V to erase the effect of the leading tone of the second dominant.

EXERCISES

1. Write and play the cadence I–IV–D/V–V_7–I in two major and two minor keys, using various dominant chords for D/V from the list given at the end of section (1).

2. Write and play the cadence I–D/IV–IV–V$_9$–I in two major and two minor keys, using the various dominant chords for D/IV.

3. Write and play the cadence I–D/IV–IV–D/V–I$_4^6$–V$_7$–I in two major and two minor keys and successively replace D/IV and D/V by the various dominants listed in section (1).

(3) : Altered Temporary Tonics

Any secondary dominant other than the second dominant usually resolves to either a *major or minor triad*, since these are *the only chords that can be heard as tonics*, whether temporary or not. In other words, neither a diminished or augmented triad nor a seven-chord can serve as a tonic. This fact is particularly important with respect to the diatonic ii°, III⁺, and vii°, for when these harmonies are tonicized, they must be appropriately altered so as to become either major or minor triads. The following are, therefore, the harmonies in diatonic Major and Minor which lend themselves to tonicization ("*" indicates an altered chord):

Major: ii, iii, IV, V, vi, vii* (Lydian)

Minor: ii* (Major), III, iv, V, VI, VII (Aeolian)

EXERCISES

Write and play the cadence I–VI–IV–II–VII–V$_7$–I in two major and two minor keys and precede each chord by a dominant, using the various secondary dominants listed at the end of section (1).

(4) : Chromaticism Due to Secondary Dominants

In C Major the secondary dominants introduce the following altered tones: C♯ (D/ii), D♯ (D/iii), F♯ (D/V), G♯ (D/vi), A♯ (D/vii), and B♭ (D/IV). In C Minor the secondary dominants introduce these tones: C♯ (D/ii), D♭ (D/VI), E (D/iv), F♯ (D/V), and A (D/VII). Consequently, the use of secondary dominants leads us into chromaticism employing all twelve tones of the scale. If tonics derived from modal mixtures are added to these harmonies of simple Major and Minor, even more colorful effects may be obtained.

When in the following additional exercises the choice of a dominant is left to the student, merely "D" is written; otherwise, a definite symbol appears.   For every "D" the student should work out at least two versions by consulting the list of possible dominants given at the end of section (1).   From the three musical examples at the beginning of this chapter it will be seen that the crucial leading tone most often appears in the bass, but this is not always necessary as the following example shows:

Beethoven — *Symphony no. 1 (beginning)*

EXERCISES

The student should write out, play, and then transpose the following exercises once on the piano, employing nonharmonic tones in them to create pleasing melodic lines of varied rhythms.

1. d   i–VI–D/IV*–IV*–D/V–V$_7$–i

2. f   i–D/ii*–ii*–VI–D/V–i$_4^6$–V$_7$–i

3. F♯   I–D/vi–vi–D/iii–iii–D/vii*–vii*–D/V–V$_9$–I

4. a   i–D/II♭–II♭–D/VI–VI–D/III–III–D/VII♮–VII♮–D/iv–iv–D/V–V$_7^{13}$–i

5. E♭   I–vi–IV–D/ii–ii–D/vi–vi–D/iii–iii–D/vii*–vii*–D/IV–IV–ii–D/V–I$_4^6$–V$_7$–IV$_4^6$–I

b : SECONDARY CADENCES

The elaboration of cadences with secondary dominants may be further
extended with the help of *secondary subdominants* so that complete
secondary cadences result, as seen in the following examples by
J. S. Bach:†

Herzlich lieb hab' ich dich   (BR 58, middle)

Schwing dich auf   (BR 142)

† In passing it should be mentioned that such cadence elaboration approaches, in fact is identical
with, modulation, except that in modulation the temporary tonic becomes more permanent by
sustaining several further cadences.

Schwing dich auf (BR 142, middle)

In the first and last measures of the first example we find secondary dominants of iii and vi, the phrase ending with a half-cadence on D/vi. In the second measure the second dominant is preceded by its own dominant (the third dominant), indicating that the passage is a secondary cadence based on the dominant (A) as a temporary tonic.   The last chord of the first measure belongs to this secondary cadence as a subdominant (vi, otherwise iii of the main key, D).

The second example is similar insofar as the secondary subdominant may also be called a harmony of the main key (III).

In the third example, however, a fully chromatic secondary double cadence appears, based on the tonicized subdominant (g).   The first two harmonies in this example can hardly be interpreted as belonging to a common key.   The second chord clearly belongs to G Minor and opens a full cadence in this key, followed by a half-cadence.

Another fine illustration of a secondary cadence is:

Mendelssohn — *Bridal March from A Midsummer Night's Dream*

As long as the basic cadence remains clearly outlined, almost any secondary cadence will be accepted by the listener. If, however, the student permits his cadence to become obscured by an abundance of chromatic chords, the entire passage will begin to sound vague. In the following exercises "S" indicates any one of the following sub-dominant chords: IV, iv, ii, ii°, ii$_7$, ii$_7^\circ$, and N6. The student should work out at least two versions of each "S" and add Roman numerals in the first three exercises.

EXERCISES

4. B♭   I–vi–IV–II$_{♭6}$/V–V$_7$/V–I$_4^6$–V$_7$–I

5. c♯   i–iv–V$_7$–i–S/VI–D/VI–VI–D/iv–iv–S/II♮–D/II♮–II♮$_6$–i$_4^6$–V$_7$–i

6. G   I–V$_5^6$–I–vi–iv$_6$(= ii/III♭)–V$_7$/III♭–III♭(= II♭/ii)–ii$_4^6$–D/ii–ii–D/V–I$_4^6$–V$_7^{13}$–I

c : DOMINANT SEQUENCES

It is easy to see how the introduction of leading tones (that is, of secondary dominants) into diatonic sequences (such as those given in exercises 1–6, pp. 178-79) will turn them into chromatic ones and make them more colorful.   In each case all one has to do is to modify every other chord so that it becomes a secondary dominant tonicizing the following harmony, which, if it is normally a diminished or augmented chord, must be appropriately altered.   The new sequences now read as given in the following exercises.

EXERCISES

Play each of the following exercises on the piano and transpose it to one other major or minor key.   In Minor use natural Minor except for the normal dominant before the last chord.   Establish the sequence motif on the second and third chords of each exercise, and repeat this motif with exactly the same fingering in stepwise descent throughout each exercise.   These exercises include the well-known Baroque sequences which Bach, among others, taught to his pupils.†   A little embroidery with nonharmonic tones turns them into excellent improvisation patterns and accompaniments for solfege and other exercises.

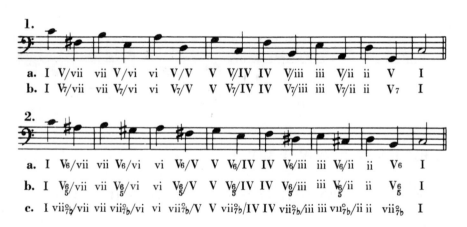

1.

a. I   V/vii   vii   V/vi   vi   V/V   V   V/IV   IV   V/iii   iii   V/ii   ii   V   I

b. I   V₇/vii   vii   V₇/vi   vi   V₇/V   V   V₇/IV   IV   V₇/iii   iii   V₇/ii   ii   V₇   I

2.

a. I   V₆/vii   vii   V₆/vi   vi   V₆/V   V   V₆/IV   IV   V₆/iii   iii   V₆/ii   ii   V₆   I

b. I   V₆₅/vii   vii   V₆₅/vi   vi   V₆₅/V   V   V₆₅/IV   IV   V₆₅/iii   iii   V₆₅/ii   ii   V₆₅   I

c. I   vii°₇♭/vii   vii   vii°₇♭/vi   vi   vii°₇♭/V   V   vii°₇♭/IV   IV   vii°₇♭/iii   iii   vii°₇♭/ii   ii   vii°₇♭   I

---

† Cf., Hans David and Arthur Mendel, *The Bach Reader* (New York: W. W. Norton & Company, Inc., 1945), pp. 395ff.

d : SECONDARY DOMINANTS WITHOUT TONICS

(1) : Successive Dominants

The basic reason for the introduction of secondary dominants is the desire to lead more forcefully into the various scale steps. The leading tones thus introduced were originally chromatic passing tones which, it was later discovered, could be pleasingly harmonized by accepted chords. As the tonal system expanded, it was found that these new chords could be accounted for as secondary dominants and subdominants.

Dominant chords are so characteristic that their implications are immediately heard even if not actually carried out. Consequently, secondary dominants are often used without resolving to their temporary tonics. One very common practice is to resolve a V_7 or vii$^{o}_{7}$♭ deceptively, not to its tonic but to its submediant or subdominant. For example:

Another common practice is to go from any form or derivative of one V_7 to that of any other, particularly one whose root is a fifth lower, as in the progression D/V–V_7–I. Actually *any* scale step may be represented by its V_7 even though the step itself does not appear in the cadence.

Of the following examples the first two show progressions of the D/V–V_7 type, and the last two show other uses of secondary dominants without tonics.

Schumann — *Album for the Young, no. 14 (end)*

V_4^7 $\begin{smallmatrix}13\\7\\3\end{smallmatrix}$ I

Chopin — *Mazurka in C-sharp Minor, no. 2 (end)*

V_5^6/V V_7 i

Chopin — *Nocturne in F Major, no. 4 (measures 12–14)*

I D/vi V_5^6 D/ii V_3^4 I

Chopin — *Etude in E-flat Major, op. 10, no. 11 (measures 48–49)*

I   iv   D/vi D/ii   D/V   V₇   I

EXERCISES

1. Write out and play the following exercises.

c. A   I–V₇–vi–vii°₇♭/ii–V₃⁴–I₆–V₂–vii–V₅⁶/iii–V₃⁴–I

d. e♭   i–V₂/V–vii₇°–V₅⁶/VII♭–V₇/ii–V₉/vii♮–vii₅♭♭°⁶/III–V₅⁶/VI–V₇–I₄₋₃

e. *Wer nur den lieben Gott*   (BR 339)

i   VI   V₇   i   D/V D/iv D/V   V   —   —   D/iv —   iv

ii   V₇   I   ii⁶₆   D/V V₇   VI   D/V   V₇   I

2. Add the Roman numerals, write out, and play the following exercise.

Befiehl du deine Wege   (BR 340)

3. Add the Roman and Arabic numerals, write out, play, and transpose the following exercise to another key.

Wie bist du, Seele   (BR 242, end)

(2) : *Further Dominant Sequences*

If we review the diatonic seven-chord sequences given at the end of Chapter 13, we see that these can now be made into the chromatic dominant sequences given in the following exercises.   These sequences must be carefully practiced.   It is easier at first to play the complete chords in the right hand together with their tonics in the left hand. The slight dissonance which results has been frequently used in music. In fact, one may stop anywhere in such sequences and with good effect resolve the dominant chord like a multiple appoggiatura to its tonic. For example, in the first sequence of exercise 1:

C V_7/IV V_7/vii V_7/iii V_7/vi   vi

EXERCISES

In the following exercises the lower notes, which represent the tonics of the indicated dominants, are to be played by the left hand.   The upper notes represent the actual bass tones of the indicated dominant chords (as in the preceding example).   Each exercise should be practiced in at least one further key.

1.

I V_7/IV V_7/vii V_7/iii V_7/vi V_7/ii V_7/V   V   I

2.

a. I	V_7/IV	V_3^4/vii	V_7/iii	V_3^4/vi	V_7/ii	V_3^4/V	V_7
b. I	V_7/IV	vii$^{\circ 6}_{5b}$/vii	V_7/iii	vii$^{\circ 6}_{5b}$/vi	V_7/ii	vii$^{\circ 6}_{5b}$/V	$\overline{V_7}$

V_3^4/IV	V_7/vii	V_3^4/iii	V_7/vi	V_3^4/ii	V_7/V	V_3^4	V_7	I
vii$^{\circ 6}_{5b}$/IV	V_7/vii	vii$^{\circ 6}_{5b}$/iii	V_7/vi	vii$^{\circ 6}_{5b}$/ii	V_7/V	V_3^4	V_7	I

3.

a. I	V_2/IV	V_5^6/vii	V_2/iii	V_5^6/vi	V_2/ii	V_5^6/V	V_2
b. I	V_2/IV	vii$^{\circ}_{7b}$/vii	V_2/iii	vii$^{\circ}_{7b}$/vi	V_2/ii	vii$^{\circ}_{7b}$/V	V_2
c. I	vii$^{\circ 4}_{3b}$/IV	V_5^6/vii	vii$^{\circ 4}_{3b}$/iii	V_5^6/vi	vii$^{\circ 4}_{3b}$/ii	V_6^5/V	vii$^{\circ 4}_{3b}$

V_5^6/IV	$V_2/$	V_5^6/iii	V_2/vi	V_5^6/ii	V_2/V	V_5^6	V_7	I
vii_{7b}°/IV	V_2/vii	vii_{7b}°/iii	V_2/vi	vii_{7b}°/ii	V_2/V	vii_{7b}°	V_7	I
V_5^6/IV	$vii_{3b}^{\circ 4}/vii$	V_5^6/iii	$vii_{3b}^{\circ 4}/vi$	V_5^6/ii	$vii_{3b}^{\circ 4}/V$	V_5^6	V_7	I

(3) : *Dominants as Scale Functions*

Continued omission of temporary tonics makes it impossible to relate all the secondary dominants aurally to their tonics. These dominants are then accepted as chords which are heard in direct reference to the main tonic. In other words, the root of such a dominant is interpreted as a diatonic step of the main key, and those tones which do not belong to the key are heard as "alterations," or nonharmonic tones:

Wolf — *To a Christmas-Rose II (Mörike Songs)*

Even the root of such a dominant chord may be heard as a nonharmonic tone. Thus an apparent paradox results: a dominant chord without a dominant function. Such "dominants" are therefore better called "major-minor seven-chords" rather than dominant seven-chords.

For instance, in the following example Vi vii is heard as an "altered" chord on the "raised" subdominant. Its root is heard as a passing tone between subdominant and dominant, and any other tones which are not diatonic are interpreted as passing or leading tones within the key as long as they do not resolve to vii:

Secondary dominants and modal mixtures (*) are combined in:

Brahms — *Der Tod, das ist die kühle Nacht (skeleton chords)*

The following exercises provide opportunities for combining secondary dominants and modal mixtures. The strangeness of some of these mixtures may be mitigated if their dominants precede them, resulting in a generally chromatic, Romantic texture.

EXERCISES

Harmonize the following melodies, play them on the piano, and check each setting with the original.

1. Schubert — *Das Wirtshaus (Winterreise, no. 21), end*

2. Schubert — *Du bist die Ruh'*

3. Schubert — *Nacht und Träume*

4. Schubert — *Morgengruss (Die schöne Müllerin, no. 8)*

iv

5. Schubert — *Die böse Farbe (Die schöne Müllerin, no. 17)*

I

6. Schubert — *Sei mir gegrüsst*

D/IIIb   IIIb   vii°7/vi   V/vi   vi

e : CHROMATIC MEDIANTS

Many effects produced by modal mixtures and secondary dominants are especially colorful because they feature successive chords with roots which are by sound (not by notation) a major or a minor third apart, such as C–E♭ (C–D♯) or C–A♭ (C–G♯), and with tones which do not all fit into one diatonic scale (for instance, an E in one chord and an E♭ in the next). Any two such chords are called *chromatic mediants*.† Because diminished and augmented triads are too ambiguous in chromatic-mediant progressions, only major and minor triads give the characteristic effect. However, any seventh or ninth may be added to such triads without disturbing the effect.

   Mediant relationships are shown schematically in the following table, in which major and minor triads are indicated respectively by capital and lower-case letters. The index numbers in this table indicate the number of chromatic relations between the two chords which are connected by a line. It should be understood that in each case we

† Also called "affinitive thirds" or "extra-tonal third-relations."

are concerned with a relationship between two chords, not one between two keys. Nevertheless, the number of chromaticisms depends on the differences between the scales represented by the two chords. For example, the E♭ triad includes two chromatic relations with the C triad (E♭ and B♭, which are not found in the C-Major scale). The chromatic relations between mediants range from zero, representing the diatonic mediants, to three. The higher an index number is, the greater will be the colorful strangeness or tension that exists between the two chords to which it refers.

Mediants of the C Major triad   *Mediants of the C Minor triad*

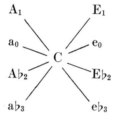   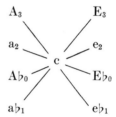

Usually the effects extracted from chromatic mediants are momentary, since they govern the progression of only two chords. Unless these chords are firmly anchored within a cadence, the use of chromatic mediants easily leads to harmonic vagueness, which may or may not be compensated for by the scintillating and attractive colors produced. Therefore, the student should not employ too many of these mediants in succession.

The color of chromatic mediants depends partly on the tonal functions of the chords involved. If we take C Major in the preceding table as the tonic, the A♭ Major and E♭ Major triads are heard as minor-major mixtures, A♭ Minor and E♭ Minor as secondary mixtures (see Chapter 16, section c), and A Major and E Major usually as secondary dominants of D Minor and A Minor. Similarly, relating to C Minor as the tonic, A Minor and E Minor are heard as major-minor functions, A Major and E Major as secondary dominants of the major-minor functions D Minor and A Minor, and A♭ Minor and E♭ Minor as secondary mixtures.

The following examples show a few uses of chromatic mediants (indicated by arrows). In the first example we see how, in order to obtain the effect of chromatic mediants, alterations are introduced that fall outside the key (here a III in Major). Such alterations usually require the replacement of a major by a minor triad, or vice versa (a secondary mixture).

Liszt — *Sonnetto 47 del Petrarca*

Liszt — *Sonnetto 47 del Petrarca (measures 43–48, skeleton chords)*

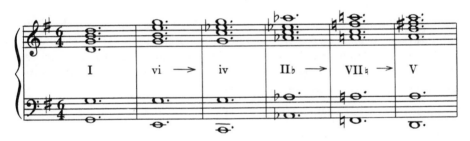

Brahms — *Immer leiser wird mein Schlummer (measures 41–47)*

EXERCISES

1. The following exercises consist of very usual cadences in which slight alterations — modal mixtures — achieve the desired effect of chromatic mediants, again indicated by arrows. Write out and play these exercises. Although root-positioned chords are most usual in chromatic-mediant progressions, use some inversions also and add a seventh occasionally.

    a. E   I → VI♮ → IV → II♮ — V — I

    b. b♭   i → vi♮ → iv → ii — V — i

    c. D   I → VI♭ → iii — V — I

    d. A♭   I — IV → II♭♭ → VII♭ → V — I

    e. f♯   i → iii♯ → II♮ → IV — VI → vii♯ → V — i

2. Further mediant effects result from the motion to any V_7 chord up or down by a major or minor third from another V_7. With the use of inversions, such progressions can be made entirely by chromatic motion when the interval is a minor third, and they are often made with the aid of a skip when it is a major third. Play the following progressions on the piano and transpose each a major third up and down:

3. Closely akin to the effect of chromatic-mediant motion is the progression of chords with roots which are at an interval of a tritone. Again both triads and seven-chords may be used:

Musorgsky — *Boris Godunov, coronation motif*

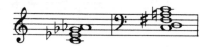

Debussy — *Ce qu'a vu le vent d'Ouest (Prelude I, 7, measures 7–9)*

Write out the following exercises, play them on the piano, and compare them with the originals.

a. Liszt — *Du bist wie eine Blume*

b. Wolf — *Gesang Weylas*

c. Duparc — *Extase (measures 5–13)*

d. Strauss — *Morgen (measures 13–38)*

19

CHROMATIC MODULATION

a : DEFINITION

Any of the chromatic procedures discussed in the preceding chapter may be employed for the purpose of modulation by leading to a chord of another key which then is firmly established through several cadences. The difference between chromatic alterations — modal mixtures, secondary cadences, and chromatic mediants — and chromatic modulation is only one of the time spent in the new key.

The Introduction of Beethoven's *Seventh Symphony* is an instructive example in this respect:

Besides numerous secondary dominants (one of them [A] introducing
a chromatic-mediant progression) and modal mixtures (which appear
in the first idea [B, B₁] and refer to the keys that characterize the
second idea), there are two modulations: the first (measure 20) is made
by way of a Minor mixture [C]; the second (measure 42), after a brief
reference to the main key (A Major) reached by way of a chromatic
mediant [D] and a return to the second key (C Major), proceeds
through a secondary dominant [E] to the third key (F Major).   Finally

(measure 52) this third key is reinterpreted as the minor submediant of the main key to bring about a return to it.

Let us recall the definition of chromatic modulation which was given in Chapter 15, section a(3): In chromatic modulations there always is a place where two successive chords must be interpreted as belonging to different keys because one of the chords contains one or several notes present in the other chord but with different accidentals (such as F in one chord and F-sharp in the other). Thus there occurs at one point a tonal break between two chords, the second of which is the modulator. There is no pivot chord.

This tonal break imbues the series of chords with color and permits quick and smooth modulations of any distance. Here again there are very many possibilities, but in order to present a basic, practical, and easily grasped technique, only those modulators will be explained in this chapter that are derived from the basic techniques of chromaticism discussed in Chapter 18: secondary dominants and chromatic mediants.

b : MODULATION THROUGH SECONDARY DOMINANTS

Any of the dominant chords listed in Chapter 18, section a(1), may be used as a modulator: V_7, V_9, V^{13}_7, vii°_7, $vii^\circ_{7\flat}$, III^+, V, and vii°. However, the last two are usually too weak. The rules for the standard resolutions of sevenths, ninths, and leading tones apply fully.

Essentially, since any V_7, $vii^\circ_{7\flat}$, and III^+ may be taken after any major or minor triad (and therefore after any seven-chord), the task is merely to find good connections. Although one may well move to any of these dominant chords (especially to any V_7 in root position) regardless of skips, it may be helpful to demonstrate how smooth connections are possible in every instance. We must remember that there are twelve different V_7 chords (one based on each tone), but only three different $vii^\circ_{7\flat}$ chords and four different augmented triads (since all other such chords can be enharmonically respelled as inversions of these three and four different chords respectively). The following table shows that a major or minor triad can be smoothly connected, that is, with half- or whole-tone steps in all voices, with (1) any V_7,

(2) any vii°$_{7b}$, and (3) any augmented triad. Sometimes it is better to double the root of the triad, sometimes to double the fifth.

The easiest and fastest way to modulate is to go directly to the dominant of the second key and to continue with the tonic and full cadence of this key. But it is equally good, and often preferable, to move to a secondary dominant of the second key, resolve it to the step tonicized by this second dominant, and use this step as the beginning of the cadence. One example will convey the general idea of chromatic modulations made with the aid of secondary dominants:

op. 1

a♭   i–iv–V–i // F (vii°₂♭/V)–V₃⁴–IV₄⁶–I

op. 3

(The // indicates the tonal break that characterizes all chromatic modulations.)   In this example the second dominant takes the place of the subdominant, and, instead of the I_4^6, the IV_4^6 strengthens the cadence.

When the modulator leads to the dominant of the second key, the cadence in the second key will always be somewhat awkward because it will be too short.   In the beginning it will therefore be better for the student to avoid such modulations and to aim rather at a harmony of the second key other than the dominant, in particular at the subdominant or one of its relatives.   Literally hundreds of such modulations are possible.

EXERCISES

1. Add Roman numerals, write out, and play the following exercises on the piano:

d.

2. Write out and play the following exercises on the piano, using various types of S and D, as well as inversions. The D in the second cadence normally includes a I_4^6.

    a. b♭ i–S–D–i // – G D/IV–IV–D–I

    b. C I–S–D–vi // – e♭ D/III–III–S–D–i

    c. D I–S–D–I–IV // – B D/vii–vii–D–IV$_4^6$–I

    d. f♯ i–S–D–i // – d D–i–S–D–i

3. Modulate through dominants in two different ways from:

    a. e to F   **c.** A to A♭

    b. b♭ to E   **d.** D♭ to g

c : MODULATION THROUGH CHROMATIC MEDIANTS

Chromatic modulations which employ a chromatic mediant as the modulator constitute a very colorful and attractive type of modulation which is one of the staples of Romantic music. Beginning with Beethoven, sections of a composition began to be linked by mediant relationships instead of dominant ones. At first the strangeness of these progressions, which included tritone progressions, was often mollified by stepwise motion, chromatic or diatonic, in most parts. But there were several other approaches. A common tone was frequently held, while the other voices skipped into the new harmony, usually after a rest. When a common tone was not available, one tone of the last chord of the first key was held for some time and then was led chromatically to a tone of the first chord of the second key, with the other tones of this chord added subsequently. Finally, composers soon discovered that fine surprise effects could be created by entering

freely into a new key which was related to the preceding one as a
chromatic mediant.   These various approaches are illustrated by the
following examples (see also Chapter 15, section a(2)).

Chopin — *Mazurka no. 33, op. 56, no. 1 (measures 78–81)* (common tone)

Chopin — *Mazurka no. 23, op. 33, no. 2 (measures 45–50)* (common tone)

Rossini — *Excerpts from William Tell Overture* (common tone in various guises)

Bruckner — *Symphony no. 4, first movement (measures 72–75)* (long-held tone)

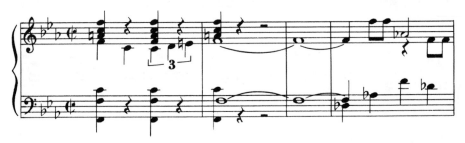

Mahler — *Symphony no. 2, first movement (measures 386–392)* (single-tone chromatic)

Beethoven — *Piano Sonata no. 13, op. 27, no. 1 (measures 12–13)* (sudden modulation)

In the following exercises the student should examine the various possibilities separately. He should keep in mind that the colorful effect of such modulations resides in the chromatic-mediant relationship between two chords and not necessarily in that between two tonics. It is quite easy, for example, to modulate from C Major to G Major by way of such mediants:

$$\text{C} \quad \text{I–IV–V–I–IV} \Big/\!\!\Big/ \text{G} \quad \text{V}_{(7)}\text{–I–IV–I}$$

In other words, this type of modulation may employ any scale steps that form chromatic mediants.

EXERCISES

Modulate on the piano with the aid of chromatic mediants in two ways from:

1. e to F

2. b♭ to E

3. A to A♭

4. D♭ to g

20

ALTERATIONS EXPRESSING
TENDENCIES OF MOTION

a : MELODIC AND HARMONIC CHROMATICISM

The purpose of all chromaticisms is either (1) to provide color contrast between chords or (2) to express tendencies in the motion from tone to tone or from key to key. Chromatic mediants are examples of the first type of chromaticism, and secondary dominants are examples of the second type. This chapter is devoted to further examples of the second type.

Tendencies of motion remain rather weak in the diatonic system. The only regular, strong tendency is that of the leading tone, with much weaker tendencies attached to other minor seconds, especially to VI–V in Minor. Modal mixtures are often employed to express additional tendencies, particularly the upward leading tone in Minor and the downward leading tones of the Neapolitan six-chord and of the minor submediant in Major.

Secondary dominants are actually the result of a desire to strengthen, or to make more explicit, the motion from one scale tone to another. Thus the effect of the second dominant, D/V, is to underscore the motion from IV through a leading tone to V; D/ii similarly reinforces the line I–II; and so on. In other words, chromaticism serves to make a motion more determined and explicit melodically, and it is interpreted harmonically as a leading-tone phenomenon, whether ascending or descending, with such leading tones normally moving on to complete the motion they imply.

Other alterations due to melodic tendencies are more recent in origin than the ones just mentioned, and they often involve a greater degree of dissonance. They affect single tones of regular chords, with the result that new chordal shapes emerge. Most frequently such alterations occur in dominants, the focus of tension in the cadence, often also in subdominants and secondary dominants. In this chapter, discussions about any chord may be applied to all of its inversions.

b · ALTERED SUBDOMINANTS

The most frequently used altered subdominant chords are ii_6 and ii_5^6 in Major with a raised sixth, which either resolves upward by a half-tone to the mediant of the key or is held over. These chords are called *augmented six-chord* and *augmented six-five-chord* respectively, and they can resolve to the following harmonies: I, I_6, I_4^6; iii, iii_6; V_7^{13}, V_2^4, $V_{5\sharp}$, $V_{5\sharp}^7$, and $V_2^{6\sharp}$ (for the last three of these see the next section), as follows:

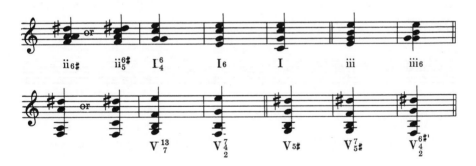

Other frequent modifications of subdominants result from passing tones leading (1) in Major from ii_7 to I_6 or iii; (2) in Minor from iv_6 and $ii^{\circ 6}_4$ to i_4^6, III_6^+, III_6, V, or v; and (3) in Major and Minor from IV_7 (iv_7) to V or I_4^6 (i_4^6). In these progressions the supertonic and/or the subdominant are raised to serve as leading tones to the following chords so that they are identical with, and may be called, secondary dominants (see the next section).   Some of the possibilities presented by these chords follow:

Similar passing tones may be employed to connect other steps as well.   In general, of the five scale steps involved in ii$_5^6$ (ii$_6$) and IV$_7$ (IV), all but the first may be chromatically altered: the second and fourth upward on the way to the mediant and the dominant respectively, and the third and sixth (in Major) downward on the way to the supertonic and dominant respectively.   Each of these alterations and any combination of them may occur, but some are better than others. The student should experiment with all these alterations.

EXERCISES

1. Add the Roman numerals, write out and play the following exercises, and transpose them a fourth up.

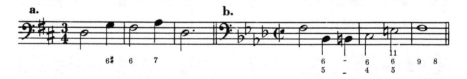

2. Write out and play the following exercises and transpose them a fourth down.

    a. a   i–ii$^{\circ\,6\sharp}_{4\,3}$–III$_6$–V$_7$–i

    b. E   I–ii$^{6\sharp}_{4\,3\,1\flat}$–I$_4^6$–V$_7$–ii$_{2\sharp}$–I

    c. B♭   I–ii$^7_{1\sharp}$–iii–ii$^{6\sharp}_{1\sharp}$–I$_4^6$–V$^{13}_7$–I

c : ALTERED DOMINANTS

(1) : Altered Triads

The simplest alterations produced by chromatic passing tones are those changing major and minor triads into augmented or diminished ones. A major triad turns into an augmented one when its fifth is raised or both its root and third are lowered. Similarly, a minor triad becomes an augmented one when its root is lowered or its third and fifth are raised. In all cases the alterations express melodic tendencies, of course, and should be treated as leading tones, as shown in the following examples:

Conversely, a diminished triad is obtained from a major one by raising its root or lowering both its third and fifth, and a minor triad becomes a diminished one by lowering its fifth or by raising its root and third:

The most frequently used altered triads are two dominant chords: the *dominant triad with raised fifth*, $V_{5\sharp}$, and the *vii° with a diminished third*, $vii°_{3\flat}$. The chords discussed in the next few pages fall into four related groups. As an aid in identifying the similarities among these chords, each family will be labeled by the same number (1, 2, 3, or 4).

1. The $V_{5\sharp}$ is an augmented triad which resolves to Major only, for its raised fifth is enharmonically identical with the mediant in Minor and cannot therefore resolve to this tone:

The only tone that may be doubled in the $V_{5\sharp}$ is the root.   The student should determine why.

2. The $vii^{\circ}_{3\flat}$, with its two leading tones (or "double leading tone") to the tonic, may resolve to Major or Minor.   This chord is called the *double-diminished triad* (also the "soft-diminished").

2a. Its first inversion is an *augmented six-chord* which is related in sound to the Phrygian triad through its bass tone (the lowered super-tonic).   The two leading tones of this dominant in form of an aug-mented six-chord (the tones which form the augmented sixth) always resolve in contrary motion to an octave (compare with the resolution of the augmented six-chord of the subdominant in section b):

The $vii^{\circ}_{3\flat}$ and its first inversion may be used wherever a V or vii° can be used.   In either chord the only tone that may be doubled is the fifth (the third of the six-chord).   Again the student should deter-mine why.

EXERCISES

1. Write out and play the following exercises and transpose them a major third up.

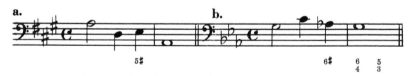

2. Write out and play the following exercises and transpose them a fourth down.

    a. D♭   I–$vii^{\circ}_{3\flat\flat}$–I–$ii^{6\natural}_{5}$–$I^{6}_{4}$–$V_{7}$–I

    b. E   I–IV–$vii^{\circ 6}_{1\natural}$–$I^{6}_{4}$–$V_{7}$–I

(2) : Altered Dominant Seven-Chords

The two essential characteristics of the V_7 chord are the major third (the leading tone) and the minor seventh. Since these two intervals may not be altered, the only tone permitting alteration is the fifth, which may be either raised as a leading tone to the mediant in Major or lowered as a descending leading tone to the tonic. Either of these altered chords may be used wherever the unaltered V_7 can stand, and in either case the dominant feeling is greatly reinforced by the additional leading tone.

1. Like the $V_{5\sharp}$ discussed in the preceding section, the V_7 *with raised fifth*, the $V^7_{5\sharp}$, can be used in Major only and normally resolves to a tonic triad with a doubled third. The interval of the diminished third between the augmented fifth and the seventh sounds poor and should be avoided. Therefore, it is best either to enlarge this interval to a tenth or to invert it into an augmented sixth. In general, the augmented fifth, as the outstanding dissonance, is most satisfactory in the soprano:

$$V^7_{5\sharp} \qquad V^6_{3\sharp}5$$

1a. In five-part settings the chord may be expanded into a ninth-chord, involving either a major or a minor ninth. Of these, the minor ninth is less successful because it sets up an additional sharpness resulting from the double-diminished fifth between the raised fifth and the minor ninth:

$$V^7_{5\sharp}9$$

2. In the V_7 *with lowered fifth*, the $V^7_{5\flat}$, which may be employed in Major or Minor, the diminished third between the third and the diminished fifth need not be avoided, but care must be taken that both

leading tones are resolved to the tonic. The diminished fifth need not always be in the soprano.

2a. The second inversion of this chord is closely related to the augmented six-chord vii$_{1\flat}^6$, (see section c(1)) and is called the *augmented four-three chord*. It is another harmony related in sound to the Phrygian triad because of its bass tone (the lowered supertonic):

$$V_{5\flat}^7 \qquad V_{\substack{4\\3\\1\flat}}$$

2b. Like the raised fifth, the flatted fifth may be incorporated in a V_9. Here, however, the major ninth is less satisfactory because it forms an augmented fifth with the altered tone:

$$V_{5\flat}^9$$

The following exercises will illustrate the uses of the various chords discussed in this section. The student should not only write out and play these exercises, but should experiment with these chords on his own in order to become more familiar with their various effects.

EXERCISES

1. A♭ I_8–$IV_{5\natural}$–ii–$V_{5\natural}$–iii–$VI\flat$–I_4^6–$V_{5\flat\flat}^7$–$IV_4^{6\flat}$–I

2. B I–$ii_5^{\cdot 6-6\text{※}}$–I_6–$vi_{6-6\natural}$–I–$V_{5\text{※}}^9$–vi_6–I

3.

4.

(3) : Altered Diminished Seven-Chords

In the vii°$_{7♭}$ either the third or the fifth may be altered.

1. The vii°$_{7♭}$, *with raised third* is related to $V^7_{5♯}$ and resolves to a major triad with a doubled third.

2. The vii°$_{7♭}$, *with lowered third*, like the $V^7_{5♭}$, resolves to Major or Minor.

2a. The first inversion of this chord, which with the lowered third in the bass is related to the Phrygian triad, is known as the *augmented six-five chord.* Here the two leading tones, the bass and the augmented sixth, must resolve into an octave. Parallel fifths are frequent in the resolution of this chord and are permitted under the name of "Mozart fifths," because that master used them often:

3. The vii°$_{7♭}$, *with raised fifth*, the vii°$^{7♭}_{5♯}$, normally resolves to Minor. This chord demands particular precautions as to the spacing of voices, for the raised fifth may set up parallel fifths with the root which are undesirable. It is therefore best either to employ inversions of this chord or, in the root position, to assign the fifth to the alto, because assigning it to the voice directly above the bass or to the soprano makes the fifths too conspicuous. In this chord it is also sometimes desirable to avoid the diminished third between the augmented fifth and the seventh by expanding or inverting that interval.

4. The vii°$_7^b$, *with lowered fifth*, the vii°$_{5b}^{7b}$, also normally resolves to Minor and demands no particular spacing of voices.

4a. The second inversion of this chord is known as the *double-augmented four-three chord* because of the double-augmented fourth it contains. It is identical in sound with the augmented six-five chord, but it resolves differently because the fourth must rise. As this chord is rather complex in notation, it is often written more simply like an augmented six-five chord with the fifth resolving upward. In this last chord the apparent fifth may therefore rise, remain stationary, or fall to a resolution:

It should further be noted that the vii°$_{3\sharp}^{7b}$ and the first inversion of vii°$_{5\sharp}^{7b}$ are enharmonically identical, as are the vii°$_{3b}^{7b}$ and the first inversion of vii°$_{5b}^{7b}$:

EXERCISES

Write and play simple I–IV–V–I cadences in G Major and E Minor and replace V successively by the various chords which have been discussed: (1) $V_{5\sharp}$, $V^7_{5\sharp}$, $vii^{o7\flat}_{3\sharp}$; (1a) $V^9_{5\sharp}$; (2) $V^7_{5\flat}$, $vii^{o7\flat}_{3\sharp}$; (2a) augmented 6, $\frac{4}{3}$, $\frac{6}{5}$; (2b) $V^{9\flat}_{5\flat}$; (3) $vii^{o7\flat}_{5\sharp}$; (4) $vii^{o7\flat}_{5\flat}$; (4a) double-augmented $\frac{4}{3}$. Transpose each exercise on the piano one whole tone up.

(4) : Augmented Six-Chords as Dominants

The four chords listed in the following table, each of which includes an augmented sixth, are known collectively as the *augmented six-chords*. Three of these chords, which have all been discussed in the preceding section, have the lowered supertonic in the bass and are related to the Phrygian triad, while the last has the lowered subdominant in the bass:

Name†	*Example*	*Symbol*	*Resolves to*
1. Augmented 6		$\overset{..}{vii}{}^{o6}_{(1\flat)}$	$I, i, VI_6, vi_6, IV^6_4, iv^6_4$
2. Augmented $\frac{4}{3}$		$V^{\;4}_{\;3}{}_{(1\flat)}$	$I, i, VI_6, vi_6, IV^6_4, vi^6_4$
3. Augmented $\frac{6}{5}$		$\overset{..}{vii}{}^{o6}_{5\flat}{}_{(1\flat)}$	$I, i, VI_6, (vi_6, IV^6_4,) iv^6_4$
4. Double-augmented $\frac{4}{3}$††		$\overset{..}{vii}{}^{o4}_{3\flat}{}_{(1\flat)}$	i_6, VI^6_4

† These chords are also known by the following irrelevant but frequently used names: number 1, "Italian sixth"; number 2, "French sixth"; number 3, "German sixth"; and number 4, "English sixth."

†† Often written like the augmented $^6_5$, with the perfect fifth instead of the double-augmented fourth, and resolving ostensibly to vi_6, IV^6_4.

The following approaches will aid in the use of the augmented six-chords:

1. The first three have the same bass tone: the lowered supertonic.

2. a. All four are very similar to each other when they share the same bass tone.   Number 1 consists of the three tones which all four chords have in common; to these three tones is added (in four-part writing) another third (above the bass tone) in number 1, a fourth (augmented) in number 2, a fifth (perfect) in number 3, and a raised fourth (double-augmented) in number 4, as follows:

b. Since the augmented sixth is aurally identical with a minor seventh, all four chords sound like root-positioned V_7 chords: number 1 incomplete (with doubled third), number 2 with lowered fifth ($V_{5\flat}^7$), and numbers 3 and 4 complete:

c. All augmented six-chords may be derived (through inversion) from a single chord, the $V_{5\flat}^{9\flat}$.   In the following figure the bracket numbers refer to the table of augmented six-chords (assuming the same spelling for numbers 3 and 4):

3. a. In all four chords the augmented sixth represents an ascending leading tone and resolves upward by a half-tone, while the bass tone is a descending leading tone (except when the chords are used as subdominants; see section b).   The bass tone of the chord of resolution is, therefore, always a half-tone lower than the bass tone of any aug-

mented six-chord (used as a dominant). The chord of resolution may be a major or minor triad, six-chord, or six-four-chord (assuming the usual combination of numbers 3 and 4 in the table of augmented six-chords), or an augmented triad.

b. The resolution of the augmented $^6_5$ to I or i deserves special comment, for it causes parallel fifths, which are accepted as "Mozart fifths."

(5) : Altered Second Dominants

All the alterations of the V_7 and its derivatives which we have discussed apply equally to secondary dominants, among which the second dominant (D/V) occupies a place of prominence. The altered second dominants in the form of augmented six-chords attracted particular attention during (and even before) the Romantic era. It was to these chords especially that the names "Italian, French, German, and English" sixths were applied. The augmented six-chords are, in fact, used more frequently as second dominants than as dominants. All that was said about these chords as dominants applies to them as second dominants, except that their bass tone is now situated a half-tone above the dominant of the key.

EXERCISES

Write and play simple cadences of the form I–D/V–D–I in four Majors and four Minors and replace D/V successively by each of the augmented six-chords, appropriately resolved: in Major to V, iii$_6$–V, or I$^6_4$–V; in Minor to V, III$^+_6$–V, or i$^6_4$–V. In order to erase the effect of the raised subdominant included in the second dominant, the dominant must always include a seventh.

d : OTHER ALTERATIONS

All the chords discussed so far in this chapter and most of those studied previously are accepted as regular chords because at some time before 1900 the tones originally introduced into them as nonharmonic tones became so familiar through frequent use that they were heard as stable chord tones. The sevenths in seven-chords were originally passing tones, the ninths and the thirteenths in the V_9 and V_7^{13} were originally appoggiaturas, and most modal mixtures and secondary dominants started out as passing-tone phenomena.

Many other alterations, however, have never been accepted as regular chord tones in the traditional system of the Classic-Romantic era. They retain their status as nonharmonic tones, expressing linear tension, and the melodic motion made explicit by them is normally followed through in music of that period. The simplest alterations of this type are strict passing and turning tones, several of which may occur simultaneously in parallel or contrary motion. A few examples will clarify their use. The student should invent a few similar progressions.

The tension of the dissonance increases with (1) the number of simultaneous chromatic motions, and (2) the degree of dissonance within the chord which contains the chromatic tones. For example,

has in both progressions four chromatic motions. The second chord, however, is very usual in sound despite its strange-looking notation. On the other hand,

includes a chord which is unusual. Although all the progressions are chromatic as in the preceding example, the tension here is stronger because of the very dissonant second chord.

Such progressions may be employed primarily as contrapuntal passages in which each line is treated with its own rhythm and melodic ornamentation, or they may be heard as the result of a chromatic melody and the "harmonization" of its separate tones. Using progression 1 in the preceding paragraph, the following elaborations provide some insight into these two techniques:

EXERCISES

1. Elaborate similarly progression 2.

2. Analyze some of the following passages:

> Richard Wagner: Beginning of the "Magic Fire Music" near the end of *Die Walküre*
>
> > Beginning of the Prelude to *Tristan und Isolde*
> >
> > Beginning of Isolde's "Love Death" near the end of *Tristan und Isolde*

César Franck: Beginning and end of the first movement of the *Violin Sonata*

Beginning of the *Symphonic Variations*

Hugo Wolf: Beginning of *Mignon II* (*Goethe Songs*)

Beginning of *Prayer* (*Mörike Songs*)

Beginning of *Ein Stündlein wohl vor Tag* (*Mörike Songs*)

e : HARMONIZATION OF CHROMATIC LINES

(1) : Single Chromatic Lines

The ear will accept any harmonization of a chromatic line as long as it is smooth, that is, as long as either half- and whole-tone progressions or dominant and mediant sequences prevail.   Needless to say, passages based only on the melodic coherence given to them by chromatic motion may lose tonal meaning, but a semblance of such meaning may be created by the use of simple chords, such as triads and seven-chords. Sections of such "floating," or "roving," suspended tonality which are brief and which begin and end on clearly recognizable tonal functions can be heard as passing-tone phenomena.   If suspended tonality is extended, however, it leads to the disregard or conscious avoidance of a tonal center and of functional harmony.

The following examples show the most usual ways in which chromatic lines are harmonized:

In general, a rising chromatic line (1), whether in the soprano, the bass, or a middle part, is most often interpreted as alternating leading tones and tonics. A descending chromatic line usually represents (2) alternating sevenths of V_7 chords or their equivalents (such as fifths of vii$_7^{\circ}$ chords) and thirds of tonics or (3) alternating diminished fifths of V_7 chords (or their equivalents) and tonics.

Other two-chord sequence motives will serve well, too, as seen in the following examples. For instance, the tones of a rising or falling chromatic line may represent (4) alternating roots and thirds of major or minor triads, or (5) roots of major six-chords (major triads in first inversion) alternating with fifths of major triads, or roots of minor six-chords alternating with fifths of minor triads.

EXERCISES

1. Play the preceding sequences 1–5 and transpose each to one other key.

2. Invent one or two new sequence patterns, harmonizing an ascending or descending chromatic line.

(2) : Two Simultaneous Chromatic Lines

Often two chromatic lines are combined in contrary motion. There are only two essentially different types of such combinations. These two types and their inversions are shown in the following examples. Their harmonizations have no tonal implications. The more one employs usual chords (triads, V_7 chords, $vii^{o}_{7\flat}$ chords), the smoother the passages will sound:

One further double-chromatic sequence is pleasing and familiar. Its starting point is a minor six-four-chord, which is followed by a V_2 and a V_7 to form a three-chord sequence motif:

EXERCISES

1. Play the preceding sequences 1–5 and transpose each to one other key.

2. Practice sequence 5 with resolutions after either the V_2 or the V_7, thus bringing the sequence to a stop.

3. Invent one or two other harmonizations of the two chromatic lines in sequences 1 and 2.

Extensive alterations cannot always be treated smoothly because of the melodic motif employed or because of a desired effect. The better known the chromatic relationships are, particularly when they have the character of dominants, the more easily can skips be employed. However, the larger the skips are, the greater the tension in the music will be. Often a pedal point will be helpful in overcoming the tonal vagueness of extended chromatic passages, whether smoothly connected or not. Chromatic passages which employ skips without a pedal point tend to obscure tonality even more radically than chromatic passages in which smooth voice leading prevails. Music by Debussy, Reger, R. Strauss, and early Schoenberg will provide many examples for analysis.

21

ENHARMONIC MODULATION

a : TOTAL AND PARTIAL ENHARMONIC CHANGE

Let us recall the definition of enharmonic modulation which was given in Chapter 15, section a(3): In enharmonic modulations there is always one chord which, through the enharmonic change of one or several (but not all) of its notes, is interpreted as belonging to two keys. Thus there is at one point a tonal break within a single chord which functions as a pivot chord.

Every tone of the octave, except G♯ (A♭), is known by three names and may be symbolized by three different notes with the aid of various accidentals. This fact is called the "enharmonic" equivalence (or identity) of notes. Playing or singing a C-sharp Major scale and a D-flat Major scale will sound exactly the same in our equal-tempered system. Such an exchange of one set of note symbols and names for another may be called *total enharmonic change* or a "simple" enharmonic change, because, when all notes are changed, the interval relationships remain unaltered.

In contrast to a total enharmonic change, *partial enharmonic change* alters the symbol or symbols for only one or a few tones while others remain unaltered, for instance, C–E♭–G and C–D♯–G. Such partial enharmonic changes reflect directional tendencies of tones. In the following example the consonant minor triad is changed to a dissonant appoggiatura-chord resolving to a major triad:

With the aid of partial enharmonic changes a vast new field of modulating devices opens up.   The riches of this new technique may well prove the undoing of the beginning composer, and restraint in the use of enharmonic changes is definitely advised.   The purpose of a modulation must always be kept in mind.   This purpose may be either (1) *tonal*, when one aims at reaching a tonality which is desired at a particular juncture because of its place in the over-all tonal scheme of a composition, or (2) *coloristic*, when one aims at producing a desired momentary effect through a chosen chord progression.   In either case the overuse of enharmonic modulation leads to boredom and vagueness. In either case, too, modulations may be given thematic meaning in order to overcome this vagueness.

As Chapters 17 and 19 dealt with the modulatory uses of the chords treated in Chapters 16 and 18, this chapter will deal with the modulatory uses of the chords discussed in Chapter 20.   As all of these express tendencies of motion through chromaticism, progression from them should be predominantly stepwise.

b : MODULATION THROUGH AUGMENTED TRIADS

The augmented triad consists of two major thirds which subdivide the octave into three equal intervals.   Consequently, the interval structure of this chord never changes in inversions, so that any inverted augmented triad sounds identical with a root-positioned one of a different spelling.   Thus in sound there are only four different augmented triads, and each may be easily reoriented and renamed.   It may also be noted in passing that these chords are derived from the whole-tone (also called six-tone, or hexatonic) scale.

Diatonically an augmented triad occurs only on III in Minor, but chromatically it can be heard as a modified major or minor triad, particularly on the dominant in Major (see Chapter 20, section c(1)). When the augmented triad is III+ in Minor, its best doubling is the third; when it is $V_{5\sharp}$ in Major, its only doubling is the root.   In either case the dominant of the key is doubled.   When the chord is heard as $V_{5\sharp}$, it resolves to I — a major triad whose root lies a half-tone above

the third of $V_{5\sharp}$. When the chord is heard as III^+, it may move to i —
a minor triad whose root lies a half-tone above the fifth of III^+—
or to V — a major triad whose root is the third of III^+. Since enharmonic changes may be made in any of the three tones of an augmented triad, the general rule is that any tone of this chord may be
used as the leading tone to either a major or minor triad or as the root
of a major triad:

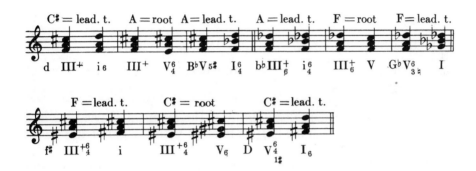

These many possible progressions render the augmented triad
very valuable for enharmonic modulation, and such modulations
usually sound satisfactory and fresh. The augmented triad which is
to serve as modulator may be reached normally as a $V_{5\sharp}$ or III^+, or
through alteration of any triad (see Chapter 20, section c(1)). As it
becomes the pivot chord, its arrangement will normally have to be
changed. One example will clarify the procedure:

EXERCISES

1. a. Write an augmented triad based on C; then change its notes enharmonically so that the chord can be successively interpreted as belonging to three keys as III$^+$ and to three keys as V$_{5\sharp}$. Determine these six keys.

  b. Do the same with augmented triads with roots on C$\sharp$, D, and E$\flat$.

2. Modulate with the aid of augmented triads from:

  a. a to f

  b. B to E$\flat$

  c. F to c$\sharp$

  d. g to F$\sharp$

  e. D to B$\flat$

  f. c to e

   If to these diatonic possibilities of the augmented triad we add the chromatic ones, the field of modulation with the aid of this chord becomes practically inexhaustible, for the augmented triad may also resolve to a minor triad rooted on any of its tones and (by half- and whole-tones only) to any seven-chord, particularly to any V$_7$. Furthermore, it is always easy to go from one augmented triad to any of the other three.

c : MODULATION THROUGH DIMINISHED SEVEN-CHORDS

Whereas enharmonic modulation through the augmented triad still retains freshness, that through the diminished seven-chord has been wrung dry. Nevertheless, it continues to be a valuable aid, particularly for piano or organ improvisation. When used in modulation, the diminished triad is heard as an incomplete diminished seven-chord. This chord consists of three minor thirds which divide the octave into four equal intervals. Consequently, the interval structure of this chord never changes in inversion, and any inversion of a diminished seven-chord sounds identical with the root position of another one. Thus in sound there are only three different diminished seven-chords, each of which is easily respelled enharmonically.

The diminished seven-chord is a leading-tone chord. It may resolve to a major or minor tonic triad (with the root a half-tone above that of the vii°$_{7b}$) or deceptively to **VI** or **iv** in Minor (with roots respectively on the seventh or fifth of the vii°$_{7b}$). The diminished seven-chord may also resolve to **V**$_7$:

$$\text{I} \qquad \text{i} \qquad \text{VI}_6 \qquad \text{iv}^6_4 \qquad \text{V}^6_5$$

Since enharmonic changes may be made in any of the four tones of the diminished seven-chord, we may resolve it to any major or minor triad (with or without a seventh) with a root which is one of the chord tones or a half-tone higher, as well as to any **V**$_7$ with a root which is a half-tone below a chord tone. Of all these resolutions, only those to the minor triads based on chord tones are somewhat weak. Considering only major and minor triads, we find that any vii°$_{7b}$ may move directly to sixteen different triads, and, through **V**$_7$ chords, to all twenty-four triads. Furthermore, any vii°$_{7b}$ moves easily to either of the other two vii°$_{7b}$ chords. The diminished seven-chord which is to serve as modulator may be reached conventionally as vii°$_{7b}$, or through smooth chromatic voice leading from any other chord.

EXERCISES

1. a. Write a diminished seven-chord based on B; then change its notes enharmonically so that the chord can be successively interpreted as vii°$_{7b}$ or one of its inversions in four different Minors (and Majors). Determine these keys.

b. Do the same with diminished seven-chords with roots on B♭ and A.

2. Modulate with the aid of vii°$_{7b}$ chords from:

a. C to g♯

b. g to D♭

c. D to f

d. A to F♯

e. e to B♭

f. b to g

d : MODULATION THROUGH THE DOMINANT SEVEN-CHORD AND ITS ALTERED FORMS

(1) : The V₇ as Modulator

The complete V_7 may be easily changed enharmonically to an augmented six-five or to a double-augmented four-three, while the incomplete V_7 and the $V^7_{5\flat}$ may be similarly changed to the augmented six- and four-three-chords (see Chapter 20, section c(4)). The V_7 of the first key is therefore a particularly colorful pivot chord for quick modulations by a half-tone downward or by a tritone:

This type of enharmonic modulation may not be reversed without sounding strained. It seems that the ear readily accepts an enharmonic change from one degree of tension to one which is equal or higher, but not to one which is lower. Thus the change from a V_7 to an augmented six-chord is smooth, but the change from the latter to the former is not. (Compare the similarly irreversible direction in the modulation through the Neapolitan six-chord, Chapter 17, section b(2).)

The possible scope of these modulations is greatly enlarged when we remember that (1) the chords of resolution need not be tonics but may represent other steps of the second key; (2) any V_7 may be reached smoothly from any major or minor triad; and (3) any V_7 may follow any other V_7. Added color may be given to any of these modulations by employing the major or minor V_9 as the pivot chord. In every case, however, care must be taken to resolve the augmented six-chord correctly.

EXERCISES

1. Write out and play on the piano:

op. 1

a. c i–S–D–i V_7
    b vii$^{\circ 6\sharp}_{5\,1\natural}$/V –D–i

op. 3

op. 1

c. A I–S–D–I V^7_5
    E♭ vii$^{\circ 6}_{5\,1♭}$ iii$_6$–ii$_7$–V$_9$–I

op. 3

op. 1

b. e♭ i–S–D–i V_7
    D V$^{4\sharp}_{3}$$^{6\sharp}_{1♭}$/V –I$^6_4$–D–I

op. 3

op. 1

d. F I–S–D–I V^8_7
    F♯ vii$^{\circ 6\sharp}_{1}$/IV –IV–V$^4_3$–I

op. 3

2. Construct, write out, and play two or three further modulations of these types.

(2) : Whole-Tone Chords as Modulators

The minor V_7^{13} is enharmonically identical with $V_{5\sharp}^7$. This identity adds a colorful possibility for switching from Minor to Major. Moreover, as both chords are derived from the whole-tone scale, further enharmonic changes may be easily made in them, with the result that these various enharmonic versions of the chord (1) may move to eight different triads:

In addition, either or both of the remaining tones of the same six-tone scale may (2) be added to the chord, turning it into a $V_{5\sharp}^9$ and $V_{\substack{9\\5\sharp}}^{11\sharp}$ respectively, or (3) replace some of its tones. One such replacement changes it to (4) a $V_{5\flat}^7$, with all its harmonic possibilities:

All these chords are impressionistic chords with a shifting, scintillating effect. They are extremely vague because of their derivation from the whole-tone scale, and they may turn in almost any direction, provided that most of their tones move chromatically or are held over into the resolving chord.

EXERCISES

1. With the aid of the chords given in the preceding examples under (1), modulate from:

    a. F to E   **b.** b to e♭   **c.** F♯ to D

2. With the aid of the chord given in the preceding example under (4), modulate from:

   a. A to E♭   **b.** g to f♯

e : MODULATION THROUGH SUBDOMINANTS

The most important subdominant chord used in enharmonic modulations is the ii$_7^\circ$ in Minor and its inversions. Although this chord has other uses in Major and Minor, it is most readily heard as a subdominant chord in Minor. In Chapter 20, section b, its altered forms were shown to be identical in sound with various forms of the V$_7$ and the augmented six-chords. Here we are therefore interested only in the unaltered form.

   At the outset it will be noted that ii$^{\circ 6}_{5}$ is enharmonically identical with vii$^{\circ 7♭}_{5♯}$ of another key and that ii$^{\circ 4}_{3}$ duplicates in sound vii$^{\circ 7♭}_{3♯}$ of another key:

In these chords any tone may be enharmonically changed and then may move chromatically up or down. The rule given in the preceding section that most or all tones should either move chromatically or be held over to the next chord applies here also, and it is the only rule that need be observed. The following example gives just a few of the many possible uses to which these chords may be put in enharmonic modulation:

EXERCISES

With the aid of the chords given in the preceding examples modulate from:

1. b♭ to e   **2.** d to B   **3.** c♯ to d   **4.** g♯ to f

22

APPENDIX TO PART III

a : RULES

(1) : Rules of Resolution

(P. 212)   The sixth of the Neapolitan six-chord resolves downward by a half-tone or a diminished third.

(P. 276)   As dominants all augmented six-chords may resolve to major or minor triads, six-chords, or six-four-chords while the bass descends a half-tone.

(2) : Rules of Modulation

(Pp. 197,201)   The best diatonic modulators are: I–vi of the lower Major for first-degree modulations and V–iii of the lower Major for second-degree modulations.

(P. 197)   When the lower Minor is involved in diatonic modulation (1) as the first key, use operation 1a — the tonic triad of the lower Major; and (2) as the second key, use operation 2a — the cadence of the lower Major.

(P. 122 ff.)   The best modulators for extended diatonic modulations are:

1. The substitution of tonic Major for Minor (or vice versa) for modulation up (or down) by three to four degrees

2. The Neapolitan six-chord of the second key for modulation up to a Minor by one to three degrees or up to a Major by four to six degrees

3. The Minor-derived iv or VI♭ in Major for modulation down by three to five degrees

(Chapter 19)   The best chromatic modulators are secondary dominants and chromatic mediants.

(Chapter 21)   The best enharmonic modulators are augmented triads, diminished seven-chords, V_7 chords (which become augmented six-chords), hexatonic chords, and ii^{o6}_5 chords.

(Pp. 258,261,286)   In most chromatic modulations the progression *to* the modulator should be as smooth as possible.   In both chromatic and enharmonic modulations the progression *from* the modulator should be as smooth as possible.

b : MEMORY AIDS

(1) : Relating to Modulation

(Pp. 189,191)   Types of modulation:

1. By skip
2. By modulator
   a. Diatonic (with pivot chords)
   b. Chromatic (without pivot chords)
   c. Enharmonic (with a pivot chord)

(Pp. 189,198)   All modulations consist of the following operations:

1. Cadence of the first key

1a. Tonic triad of the lower Major (in diatonic modulation with the lower Minor as the first key)

2. Modulator (missing in modulations by skip)

   2a. Cadence of the lower Major (in diatonic modulations with the lower Minor as the second key)

3. Cadence of the second key

(2) : *Relating to the Modes*

(P. 206 ff.)   The Church modes differ from Major and Minor as follows:

$$\begin{aligned}
\text{Dorian (on D)} &= \text{Minor} + 1 \text{ accidental} \\
\text{Phrygian (on E)} &= \text{Minor} - 1 \text{ accidental} \\
\text{Lydian (on F)} &= \text{Major} + 1 \text{ accidental} \\
\text{Mixolydian (on G)} &= \text{Major} - 1 \text{ accidental}
\end{aligned}$$

(P. 207)   The characteristic intervals of the Church modes are:

   The Dorian (major) sixth (in Minor)
   The Phrygian (lowered) second
   The Lydian (augmented) fourth
   The Mixolydian (minor) seventh (in Major)

(P. 212)   The Neapolitan six-chord is (1) a major six-chord with IV as the bass tone, and (2) the first inversion of a major triad on II♭.

(3) : *Relating to Chromaticism*

(Chapters 16, 18, and 20)   The types of chromaticism are:

1. Modal mixtures
2. Tonicization
3. Chromatic mediants
4. The creation of leading tones (expressing melodic tendency)

(P. 267 ff.)   The most common altered chords are:

1. Subdominants: $\text{iv}_{6\sharp}$ (augmented six-chord)
                          $\text{ii}^{\circ 6\sharp}_{5}$ (augmented six-five chord)

2. Dominants: $V_{5\sharp}$, $vii^{o6}_{1\flat}$ (augmented six-chord; Italian sixth)

$V^7_{5\sharp}$, $V^7_{5\flat}$ (including the augmented four-three chord; French sixth)

$vii^{o7\flat}_{3\sharp}$, $vii^{o7\flat}_{3\flat}$ (including the augmented six-five chord; German sixth)

$vii^{o7\flat}_{5\sharp}$, $vii^{o7\flat}_{5\flat}$ (including the double-augmented four-three chord; English sixth)

INDEX